ISSUE 10, OCTOBER 2020

AUSTRALIAN FOREIGN AFFAIRS

Contributors

Allan Behm is head of the international and security affairs program at The Australia Institute, Canberra.

Sophie Chao is a postdoctoral research associate at the University of Sydney.

Renée Fry-McKibbin is a professor of economics in the Crawford School of Public Policy at the Australian National University.

Patrick Lawrence is an American essayist, critic, lecturer and former Asia-based correspondent, and the author of five books.

Timothy J. Lynch is associate professor in American politics at the University of Melbourne.

Rory Medcalf is a professor and head of the National Security College at the Australian National University.

Karen Middleton is *The Saturday Paper*'s chief political correspondent.

Primrose Riordan is the South China correspondent at *The Financial Times*.

Hugh White is an emeritus professor of strategic studies at the Australian National University.

Australian Foreign Affairs is published three times a year by Schwartz Books Pty Ltd. Publisher: Morry Schwartz. ISBN 978-1-76064-2051 ISSN 2208-5912 ALL RIGHTS RESERVED. No part of this publication may be reproduced, stored in a retrieval system, or transmitted in any form by any means, electronic, mechanical, photocopying, recording or otherwise, without the prior consent of the publishers. Essays, reviews and correspondence © retained by the authors. Subscriptions – 1 year print & digital auto-renew (3 issues): $49.99 within Australia incl. GST. 1 year print and digital subscription (3 issues): $59.99 within Australia incl. GST. 2 year print & digital (6 issues): $114.99 within Australia incl. GST. 1 year digital only auto-renew: $29.99. Payment may be made by MasterCard, Visa or Amex, or by cheque made out to Schwartz Books Pty Ltd. Payment includes postage and handling. To subscribe, fill out the form inside this issue, subscribe online at www.australianforeignaffairs.com, email subscribe@australianforeignaffairs.com or phone 1800 077 514 / 61 3 9486 0288. Correspondence should be addressed to: The Editor, Australian Foreign Affairs, Level 1, 221 Drummond Street, Carlton VIC 3053 Australia Phone: 61 3 9486 0288 / Fax: 61 3 9486 0244 Email: enquiries@australianforeignaffairs.com Editor: Jonathan Pearlman. Deputy Editor: Julia Carlomagno. Associate Editor: Chris Feik. Consulting Editor: Allan Gyngell. Digital Editor and Marketing: Georgia Mill. Editorial Intern: Lachlan McIntosh. Management: Elisabeth Young. Subscriptions: Iryna Byelyayeva. Publicity: Anna Lensky. Design: Peter Long. Production Coordination: Marilyn de Castro. Typesetting: Akiko Chan. Cover photograph by Manan Vatsyayana / Getty. Printed in Australia by McPherson's Printing Group.

FRIENDS, ALLIES AND ENEMIES

Australia faces serious challenges as it seeks security and prosperity in a contested Asia, but the main problem is clear and agreed: how to handle the risks an assertive China poses as America's dominance in the region wanes. The solution seems equally obvious – instead of relying on the United States as the sole guarantor of the nation's security, Australia will need to find new, like-minded partners to push back against China and compensate for any decline in US relative power.

Indeed, almost every recent foreign policy document or speech by the Australian government contains this prescription. Here is Scott Morrison addressing the Aspen Security Forum on 5 August:

> 'The jungle is growing back,' as Robert Kagan has observed. And we need to tend to the gardening. A critical priority is to build a durable strategic balance in the Indo-Pacific. For more like-minded nations to act more cohesively, more consistently, more often. To align.

Here is Australia's foreign minister, Marise Payne, addressing the Australian National University on 16 June: "As the distribution of wealth and power has shifted, Australia has been deepening our ties to nations who share our vision of a region and a globe that promotes peace and prosperity for all, under an international order built around rules."

And here is the Defence Strategic Update, released on 1 July:

[H]abits of cooperation in the Indo-Pacific are being challenged, leading to uncertainty and complicating security partnerships. This is why Defence will continue to work to strengthen defence and diplomatic ties with the countries in Australia's immediate region, working alongside important partners such as the United States, Japan and New Zealand.

The path for Australia might sound refreshingly simple and uncontentious. But it raises serious questions.

First, is this plan actually viable? An answer will involve considering who are Australia's potential partners in the region, what types of commitments they will be willing to make and whether to pursue traditional alliances with single states or to form small coalitions, in which the collective heft is greater but the commitments may be looser.

In addition, finding partners is not as easy as it may seem, since countries in the region hold differing views of China and vary widely in readiness to confront Beijing. In July 2019, for instance, Australia joined twenty-one countries in issuing a condemnation of China's mass detention of Uyghurs; the only other signatory in the Indo-Pacific was New Zealand. Among the more than fifty countries that, days later, issued a statement defending China, at least five were regional neighbours: Cambodia, Laos, Myanmar, Nepal and the Philippines. Australia does not, like South Korea or Japan, stare at China across a sea; nor is it one of the many claimants to disputed territory in the South China Sea. Each country in the region has unique interests and qualities, which are likely to stretch the limits of the term "like-minded".

But the other problem with Canberra's plan is that its rhetoric has been so at odds with its action. Canberra has cut aid to South-East Asia and reduced funding to the Department of Foreign Affairs and Trade, whose diplomats would presumably be required to pave the way for these new crucial partnerships. And the government shows little sign that it is willing to view countries in the region as genuine, trusted partners. When Scott Morrison tried to muster support for an independent inquiry into the origins of COVID-19, he called Donald Trump, Angela Merkel and Emmanuel Macron – but no leaders in Asia.

Yes, Australia has diagnosed its problem. But the remedy may not be as simple as proposed – the premises, and feasibility, of making new friends and seeking new allies need to be tested.

Jonathan Pearlman

GREAT EXPECTATIONS

Can Australia depend on its neighbours?

Hugh White

For half a century, Australian strategic policy has shifted uneasily between two poles: self-reliance in the defence of Australia, and the closest possible alignment with and dependence on the United States. But the Australian government's 2020 Defence Strategic Update, released in July, marks an important change in direction. Both approaches are largely abandoned, and instead, Australia will seek its security principally as part of a coalition of Asian countries. The government plainly hopes that this coalition will be led by the United States, but that is not taken for granted. We no longer repose our trust in America alone, and if America fails us then we will look not to ourselves but to our Asian neighbours – as John Curtin might have put it, "free of any pangs". This raises critical questions. Can Australia credibly depend on our Asian neighbours for our security? What are the alternatives?

The government's abandonment of self-reliance as the country's primary strategic objective is a particularly stark change. Every defence policy statement from 1976 to 2013 has declared this to be Australia's highest priority. The 2016 Defence White Paper steps back from that by stating that defending Australia is one of three core missions, along with contributing to operations in Maritime South-East Asia and the South Pacific, and to global coalitions. Self-reliance is hardly mentioned. But this year's update goes much further. It makes no mention of the defence of Australian territory specifically. We are left to assume that Australia falls within the expansively defined "immediate region" – covering everything from New Zealand to the borders of India and China – which is the new focus of Australian defence planning. The priority, it seems, is to build forces to fight alongside other countries to defend stability and order across this region. Likewise, self-reliance is only mentioned in relation to the ill-considered idea to put deterrence at the heart of Australia's defence posture. Thus, decades of commitment to developing and sustaining the capacity to defend Australian territory independently from direct attack have been summarily jettisoned.

At several points the update dutifully reiterates Canberra's commitment to the US–Australia alliance and its confidence in America's role in Asia, but the alliance is no longer accorded the unique status it has held for so long in Australia's strategic posture. Instead, it is listed merely as one of several important relationships. For example, the foreword refers to strengthening engagement with "the

United States, Japan, India, ASEAN and other allies and partners in our region". More tellingly, the opening of Chapter 2 refers to the development of strategic relations with countries in our region – not until paragraph 2.7 is there any substantial reference to the United States, and that says merely that priority will be given to cooperating with America in the immediate neighbourhood. Nowhere is there a clear and sustained description of the overriding significance of the US–Australia alliance of the kind that was set out over more than three pages in the 2016 Defence White Paper.

The impression that Australia is de-emphasising its alliance with the United States is amplified by the limits placed on Australia's willingness to support America. In contrast to the 2016 White Paper, which gave equal priority to operations throughout Asia and globally, the update stipulates that commitments in North Asia, as well as in the Middle East and elsewhere, have lower priority than those within the immediate region. The downgrading of North Asia is especially significant, because that is where America faces its most serious flashpoints with China and would most earnestly seek Australia's support. The update seems to be warning the United States not to expect Australian support in a war with China over Taiwan. Canberra's apparent downgrading of the relationship with Washington is reinforced by the fact that, in June, Minister for Foreign Affairs Marise Payne delivered a major speech offering an overview of Australia's foreign policy and failed to mention the United States once. That, surely, is a first.

Anxieties in Asia

It is easy to understand why the government is stepping back from these two enduring pillars of Australian strategic policy. The reason is China, which the update plainly identifies as the major source of risk in the decades ahead. Not since the late 1960s has an Australian government so bluntly named China a potential military peril. China's re-elevation to a strategic threat changes everything.

Take self-reliance. The idea that Australia could defend itself independently only began to look credible in the early 1970s, as fear of China evaporated. The nation had loomed as Australia's primary threat throughout the 1950s and 1960s, until Whitlam's and Nixon's openings to Beijing

America's ability to ensure Australia's security can no longer be taken for granted

in 1972. Indonesia then became the only country that could present even a remotely credible military challenge, and it became for decades the unstated but unmistakable focus of Australian defence policy. That made defence self-reliance achievable, because Indonesia's air and naval forces have always been weak. But China has the capacity to seriously contest Australia's air and naval superiority in its maritime approaches. No government has ever suggested that Australia should aspire to defence self-reliance against the more serious kinds of attack that China could launch in the decades ahead. Most among Australia's strategic policy community assume it would be impossible. So as China looms again, now much more powerful than it was in the 1960s, the government is abandoning self-reliance and returning to the idea that Australia must rely on others in defending against threats that seem too big to confront alone.

As China rose in the late 1990s and early 2000s, it seemed natural and even inevitable that Australia would look to the United States for protection, and be willing to do more to support them in return. This was an important theme in the Howard government's 2000 Defence White Paper, in which the capability to contribute forces to a US-led coalition in a war with China began to weigh alongside the demands of self-reliance against Indonesia. Since then, and notwithstanding the distractions of the War on Terror, many major defence investment decisions have been made with this imperative in mind. By the time the 2016 White Paper was published, it was clear – if not explicit in the document itself – that supporting America in a war against China had become the primary strategic objective of Australia's defence forces. It was confidently assumed in Canberra that Washington would be successful in confronting and containing any Chinese threat to Australia or to the regional order.

Now that confidence has been shaken. The most obvious reason is Donald Trump. His America First isolationism, his dysfunctional policy and diplomatic processes, his seeming partiality for Xi and his focus on China as an economic rather than a strategic rival all raised early doubts that America would be the bulwark against Beijing that Canberra expected. But while Washington's eagerness to confront

China has since increased, with bold talk of a "new Cold War", its capacity to do so successfully looks less and less certain. China is a formidable rival. Its economy – far bigger relative to America's than the Soviet Union's ever was – makes it the most powerful adversary America has ever faced. Its massive and strategic investment in maritime forces has undermined US military superiority in the Western Pacific. Its huge trade and investment footprint give it immense diplomatic leverage. And it is deeply resolved to take America's place as the leading power in East Asia.

Nearly three years after declaring China to be its key strategic rival, Washington still has no coherent policy to resist this challenge. The reasons go deeper than the failings of the Trump administration. They go to the fundamental question of whether America needs to preserve its leadership role in Asia enough to justify the costs and risks of containing a rival as powerful as China in China's own backyard. China's strength and resolve means those costs and risks will be high. Many US policymakers still underestimate all this, assuming they can face down China without breaking a sweat. They may not be so keen to wage a new Cold War when the costs of lost economic opportunities and increased defence spending, and the clear risks of major war, become clear. American voters may be even less keen. So even after the pandemic, and even under a more effective president than Trump, America's ability to contain China's ambitions in Asia and ensure Australia's security over the decades to come can no longer be taken for granted. And in the short term, there is a real risk that miscalculations in Washington could spark a confrontation with China that America cannot win and that might well lead to a catastrophic regional war.

These are anxious times. Not since early 1942 have Australians felt so in need of allies, yet been so unsure of their major ally. It is not surprising, then, that Canberra is eagerly, even desperately, looking for new protectors.

The allure of an Asian NATO

At first glance, our Asian neighbours seem promising partners. We live in a region full of countries that share our concerns about China. Some of them are already powerful, while others have clear potential, and they are well placed within the region to try to counter China's ambitions. It makes sense to consider how they might help to keep us secure in the decades ahead.

The obvious idea is to use their strength to buttress America's dwindling power and resolve, drawing them together into a regional US-led coalition to contain China. In other words, an Asian NATO. The implied analogy with America's Cold War alliance in Europe to contain the Soviets is imprecise, as we will see. But the label seems apt when so many in Washington, and Canberra, see the contest with China as a new Cold War.

The germ of this idea can be traced back almost twenty years. Before that – when Australia first began to engage with Japan and South Korea on strategic questions in the 1990s – Washington was distinctly cool on pursuing closer interaction between the spokes of its "Hub and Spokes" alliance structure in Asia (America the hub, and its regional allies Australia, Japan, South Korea, Thailand and the Philippines the spokes). But in the 2000 presidential election campaign, Republicans began to argue that China should be seen as a competitor rather than a partner, and in its first months the Bush administration cast around for ideas about what to do about China. In early 2001, for example, a high-profile neo-conservative US think tank, Project for the New American Century, invited experts from several Asian democracies to discuss how they could respond collectively to curb China's growing influence. The issue was swamped by 9/11, but it bobbed

Asian countries will pay dearly if they dare to support US efforts to contain China

up again in 2002 with the initiation of a trilateral security dialogue between America, Australia and Japan. In 2007, Japan's prime minister, Shinzō Abe, launched the Quad, a security dialogue that included India as its fourth member. Canberra soon sunk the initiative, worried about Beijing's response. Yet by 2011 – the year Obama announced America's Pivot to Asia – the idea of a regional coalition had reappeared in the concept of the Indo-Pacific. The Quad was revived in 2017. Today, a US-led Indo-Pacific alliance to contain China seems to many to have the irresistible force of an idea whose time has come.

The underlying rationale for a form of Asian NATO is simple enough. Countries throughout Asia fear China's rising power and its evident ambition to become the regional hegemon. They welcome America's role in preventing Chinese dominance by balancing China's power and limiting its influence. It therefore seems obvious that they will be eager to cooperate to support America in doing that. To many, the geopolitical logic appears so strong as to seem self-evident, and the idea has obvious appeal to a generation of US policymakers for whom the success of NATO in defeating the Soviets looms large.

But the reality is that the notion is still very vague and ill-defined. It is easy to agree that China's neighbours are all anxious about its growing reach, but much harder to say what they are prepared to do about it. Broad gestures of diplomatic support don't thaw much ice in a Cold War. China is determined to restore its position as the primary power in East Asia, and will bitterly resent and savagely punish those who oppose it. It has the capacity to impose high costs on its weaker neighbours at relatively low cost to itself. Asian countries will pay dearly if they dare to support US efforts to contain China. So while they might like to see China contained, it is unlikely they will be willing to contribute towards this containment.

That is clearest when it comes to collective military action. Advocates of collective action often imply that the action they have in mind is largely diplomatic. But China won't be contained by diplomacy alone. America and China are competing to determine which will hold sway over the world's most dynamic and prosperous region: these are the kind of stakes for which great powers have, throughout history, gone to war. That does not make war inevitable, but it does mean that each side will try to use the threat of war to convince the other to back off – just as the Americans and the Soviets did in the Cold War.

The threat of force is central to China's campaign to displace America. That is why it has done so much to build up its military. America must reciprocate, because nothing short of a credible threat to respond in kind will deter China. That means convincing the Chinese that America is willing to fight a full-scale regional war. An Asian regional coalition will only be effective in helping America resist China's bid for primacy if it contributes substantially to that threat. In other words, there must be a real strategic alliance, like NATO, and its members must be willing to go to war with China to achieve the alliance's aims. In this context, Frederick the Great's aphorism that diplomacy without arms is like music without instruments is correct.

Can that kind of alliance be built in Asia? One way to explore this question is to look back to the last time something similar was attempted. Few now recall that there was an Asian NATO in the early decades of the Cold War. It was called SEATO: the South East Asia Treaty Organization, established under the Manila Treaty, signed in 1954 by America, Britain, France, Australia, New Zealand, Pakistan, the Philippines and Thailand. It was designed to contain the communism in the region – especially communist China.

SEATO was a big deal in its day, seen by many as the key to our region's security. From the mid-1950s to the late 1960s it loomed larger in Australian strategic policy than the ANZUS Treaty. The Menzies government cited SEATO when it committed troops to combat operations in Vietnam in 1965, for example. But its members never acted together effectively to resist China's ambitions, and it was wound up ignominiously in 1977.

SEATO failed strategically because its members' interests and objectives did not converge sufficiently to compel them to accept the costs and risks of cooperative military action. Britain and France – then as now – had more pressing priorities closer to home. The Asian members were fragile and uncertain. Australia and New Zealand were relatively weak and, in a series of crises in the late 1950s and early 1960s, proved unwilling to back America's eagerness to confront China directly. It was never very clear to America's SEATO allies that preventing China from overrunning Taiwan or Laos was important enough to justify a major war. The contrast with Western Europe was stark: for all the differences that bedevilled NATO over the decades before 1989, it was never in doubt that the security of all its members really did depend on defending the line of the Iron Curtain.

SEATO also made little operational sense. Discussions about geopolitics often overlook operational issues – questions about how military force might actually be used – but these are essential because they determine countries' strategic choices. The operational realities for SEATO were shaped profoundly by East Asia's geography. For centuries it has been predominantly a maritime theatre. The outside powers – European and American – that have controlled the region for so long have done so with maritime strength. Accordingly, resisting China's challenge to US power in the 1950s and 1960s turned out to be a maritime contest. US efforts to extend control onto the East Asian continent – Korea and Vietnam – were costly failures. But America's overwhelming superiority in the air and at sea allowed it to dominate nonetheless, leading to Mao's acceptance of US regional primacy in 1972. Since then, America has upheld the regional order primarily with maritime power. Only the Korean Peninsula has substantial US ground forces.

This is very different from the situation in Europe, where America had little choice but to confront the Soviet Union in a contest for continental control. To prevail, America had to rely

India has the potential to transform the strategic weight an Asian NATO would bring

on its European allies for two things. First, it needed their forces, because America lacked the capability to wage a large-scale solo land campaign against massive Soviet forces. That required the commitment of allied forces and extremely elaborate command and logistics arrangements between the allies. Second, these allied forces needed to be able to fight across one another's national borders throughout Western Europe. None of this would have been possible without the kind of close collective defence commitments that NATO enshrined.

By contrast, as became clear after 1972, America didn't need to confront China on the Asian mainland to achieve its goals in the region. It needed only to preserve its maritime superiority in the Western Pacific. America still required allies, but for different reasons than in Europe. It had no need of its allies' armed forces, because its air and naval strength could easily defeat any challenge. Nor did it need its allies to cooperate with one another. All it really sought from them were bases for US maritime forces. This was established in a set of bilateral arrangements with key countries – especially Japan and the Philippines. So SEATO collapsed both because its members' objectives didn't align and because it wasn't essential to Washington.

This prompts two important questions about the prospects for an Asian NATO in the decades ahead. Strategically, do the objectives of China's Asian neighbours converge strongly enough with America's and with one another's to provide the essential basis for an alliance? And operationally, would a coalition of Asian allies do much to help America confront and contain China's challenge? The answer to both questions is probably not.

The cost of confronting China

China's neighbours fear its growing power and ambitions, but do they fear it enough to drastically impair their relations with Beijing by joining a close-knit coalition against it? And to commit to war with China if one among them is attacked? It is far from clear that they do.

China doesn't – at least so far – pose the kind of threat to most of its neighbours that the Soviet Union did during the Cold War.

Politically, the Soviets aimed to impose a communist system on other countries and were supported by powerful forces within many of those countries. China seems only to want other nations to respect its interests. Militarily, immense Soviet forces in Eastern Europe posed a very real threat of invasion to Western Europe, and Europe's compact continental geography meant that a Soviet attack on Germany, for example, directly increased the threat to France and Britain. China's military, though it has grown substantially, does not pose the same kind of threat to its neighbours, and Asia's diverse maritime geography means that a Chinese attack on one country does not directly increase the threat to others. Above all, unlike the Soviets, China offers vital economic opportunities, which countries are very reluctant to forgo.

Nor do China's neighbours all share America's objectives in Asia. Washington wants to preserve US primacy in the region, while most Asian nations just want to avoid Chinese hegemony. They want America to stay in Asia to balance China, not to dominate it, and they will calibrate their support accordingly – as Singapore's prime minister, Lee Hsien Loong, made clear in a June 2020 essay in US journal *Foreign Affairs*. Moreover, their willingness to support America against China will depend a lot on their confidence in America's own commitment to the cause, and this has inevitably been shaken for the same reasons Australia's has.

Doubts about the viability of an Asian alliance against China are highlighted by India's position. It is no coincidence that the most fervent promoters of an anti-China alliance are those keenest to expand the Asia-Pacific region by bringing in India. Their concept of the Indo-Pacific expresses the hope that India will join the alliance and help to contain China's influence throughout Asia. India's participation has the potential to transform the strategic weight an Asian NATO would bring to the contest with China. By 2030 its economy will likely be bigger than the rest of Asia's combined (excluding China), and approaching America's. Its gross domestic product is predicted to be nearly half the size of China's, while Asia's second- and third-largest economies – Japan and Indonesia – will total only one-eighth.

But will India play? That depends mostly on China. The more aggressively China tries to dominate India and its surrounds, the more reason India will have to align with America and other Asian countries. If China is smart enough to moderate its ambitions in South Asia and the Indian Ocean, where India seeks preponderance, India will have little reason to challenge China's ambitions in East Asia and the Western Pacific. We would be unwise to assume that Beijing will do Washington, Tokyo and Canberra a big favour by forcing Delhi into their arms. And we would be equally unwise to assume that India would oppose Chinese domination of East Asia as long as it could dominate South Asia. So while Delhi has been happy to be wooed by Washington and its allies, it shows no sign of being willing to make serious commitments to confront China beyond its own close region.

Optimists about the prospects for an Asian alliance against China often argue that its strength will spring from shared values – freedom, democracy, the rule of law and so on. But how far do our Asian neighbours' values really align? Think of Vietnam, with a communist government just as authoritarian as China's, or indeed India, whose democratic political system nonetheless encompasses some highly repressive policies against minorities. And countries seldom act to promote their values at significant cost to their interests. Australia, for example, has been willing to incur mild Chinese displeasure over its stance on Hong Kong or Uighur detentions, but it has not been willing to risk much greater damage to its interests by infringing Beijing's One China policy over Taiwan. Other countries make similar calculations. If shared interests do not drive Asian countries to cooperate effectively to contain China, we would be unwise to expect that shared values will.

It would be very risky to expect that Australia can look to an alliance of like-minded neighbours

So much for the prospects of an Asian alliance at the strategic level. A whole separate set of questions arise when we ask how it could work at the operational level. How much help could the members of an alliance realistically offer one another in a conflict with China? Asia has a sharp division between continental and maritime spheres. The maritime powers include America, Japan and India (the Himalayas makes India's land border with China impassable for large-scale forces, so they confront each other primarily as maritime powers). These countries could do little to help China's smaller mainland neighbours resist military pressure from Beijing. America's sorry experiences in Korea and Vietnam attest to the difficulty of fighting land wars in Asia, and those problems are amplified by China's growing ability to interdict military deployments to Asia by sea or air. So there is little that America, Japan, India or Australia could do to help Vietnam, Thailand or even South Korea resist a Chinese attack.

It seems more credible that the maritime powers could help one another. America's formidable air and naval forces could assist Japan or India to defend a Chinese attack by inhibiting Chinese power-projection operations. But this is less important to Japan or India than one might expect. Long-term trends continue to make it easier to find and sink ships than to defend them. That shifts the advantage to those defending against power-projection operations. Japan and India, despite being weaker than China, do not need to rely on the United States to defend them from Chinese maritime power because they can do it for themselves – especially if they have an independent nuclear deterrent as well. Even smaller countries such as Australia might be able to do this, as I argue in my book *How to Defend Australia*. So Asia's maritime powers don't really need America. Nor do they need one another. In the maritime domain, they can stand alone. That means there is much less reason to take on costly and risky alliance commitments.

The same operational realities mean that Asia's maritime powers cannot do much to help America win a Western Pacific war with China.

In that kind of war, America would have to project power against China by sea, and China would enjoy the advantages of defence, allowing it to largely deny the Western Pacific to US forces. The result would be a costly stalemate at the operational level, which would read as a Chinese win at the strategic level. Regional allies could increase the costs of the conflict to China, but they could not change the course of events sufficiently to deliver a swift, cheap US victory. So an Asian NATO would do little for America in reducing the costs and risks of a new Cold War against China. Awareness of that fact means China's neighbours are less likely to feel sure of America's support. Without a strong operational rationale, an Asian NATO looks even more improbable.

The conclusion is clear. In the more contested and militarised environment of coming decades, in which the government itself acknowledges that Australia faces an increased probability of high-intensity conflict, it would be very risky to expect that Australia can look to an alliance of like-minded neighbours led by the United States as the basis for its security. Nor, in the likely event that Washington steps back from any major role in Asia, can we prudently expect to rely on such an alliance without the United States. All the reasons why an Asian NATO with the United States would be hard to sustain apply equally to an alliance without it. Every country in Asia faces a choice between living with China's growing reach and influence and doing what would be necessary to oppose its ambitions. Joining an alliance to oppose China would carry the costs of lost economic opportunities and the risks of major war. Countries are unlikely to take on those costs and risks unless they feel existentially threatened by China's ambitions – the way Western Europeans felt threatened by the Soviets during the Cold War – rather than anxious and uneasy, as they do now. And even if their anxieties grow, they will not commit to an effective alliance unless they are reasonably sure that others will commit too. Neither of these conditions seems likely to be fulfilled.

We can test this judgement by reflecting on how readily Australia would accept the costs and risks of an alliance against China. Would we be willing to contribute forces to support Japan in a war over the Senkaku/Diaoyu Islands? To support India in a clash in the Indian Ocean? To support America in a military conflict over Taiwan? The government itself seems unsure, as we see in the way it downplays the prospect that Australia might contribute forces to conflicts in North Asia in the 2020 Defence Strategic Update.

Similarly, how readily would these countries come to our aid in a major crisis? How sure could we be that Japan or India or Vietnam would sacrifice their relationship with China and risk war with such a powerful close neighbour to help Australia if a confrontation over a Chinese base in the South-West Pacific escalated into a military clash? Certainly, they would not feel compelled to do so by the hope that Australia would return the favour if they were threatened by China, because Australia would not have forces to offer any significant help. In the world of power politics, how much help you can expect from an ally depends a lot on how much the ally can expect you to help them.

In defence of a self-reliant Australia

The more closely one examines the government's hopes for a new regional coalition, the less viable the whole idea seems. Militarily, the defence policy outlined in the update assumes that Australia can take on a vast array of new alliance commitments to fight in high-intensity conflicts with an adversary as powerful as China without substantially increasing the forces we have been planning and developing for decades. Despite the claims made when it was launched, the update contains no commitments to significantly expand Australia's defence capabilities, nor to reconfigure them for the new operational demands our strategic aspirations would impose on them. Most tellingly, there is no commitment to substantially increase the defence budget.

Australia must make its way alone, and take responsibility for its own security

The government suggests that Australia faces the most dangerous outlook since the 1930s, yet plans to spend only the same share of GDP on defence considered barely adequate in the optimistic 1990s.

This curious complacency is also clear in the government's diplomatic plans. Several passages in the update describe the steps that Canberra will take to deepen and strengthen Australia's defence and strategic relationships with Asian neighbours. It's striking that nothing proposed goes beyond what has already been done for years, even decades. Since the 1950s Australia has been building defence relationships with Asian countries; since the early 1990s it has been active in helping to develop regional multilateral security fora; and since about 2002, as we have seen, it has been tentatively exploring a collective regional response to China, toying with closer contact with India and Japan. But none of this has produced anything that looks remotely like the foundations of the kind of regional alliance that the government seems to be relying on for Australia's future security.

How little has been achieved is shown by India's refusal for many years, and despite earnest pleas from Canberra, to invite Australia to take part in the annual Malabar naval exercises it conducts with Japan and the United States. How little is being attempted is shown by how eagerly Australia seized on the news that it might be invited this year. An invitation to Malabar would not give Australia any reason to expect that India will help us deal with China, and we'd be naive to imagine it did. Building the kinds of relationships that deliver effective mutual commitments requires a long-term, full-scale diplomatic campaign of the kind we have not seen from Canberra for a very long time. If it was serious about this approach, we would expect a lot more energy, imagination and effort put into building new alliances than has been evident so far. So perhaps it is not serious.

That is a little shocking, because the government is right to say that Australia faces higher risks in the decades ahead than it has faced since the 1960s and arguably the 1940s. So what should it be doing to prepare for the looming perils? The answer is simple but not easy.

First, the government should acknowledge that for the first time in our history, as Western power in Asia is finally eclipsed, Australia must make its way alone, and take responsibility for its own security in a way it has never had to before. Rather than stepping away from defence self-reliance as things get tougher, we must step into it.

Second, Australia should work to build the strongest linkages it can with the countries that could be of most value in the decades ahead. That means abandoning unrealistic ambitions for strategic partnerships with every country between Australia and China. Instead, Canberra should focus on the countries whose strategic interests converge most closely with Australia's, which Australia can most assist and which can most assist Australia. On all these counts, our neighbours in maritime South-East Asia stand out, especially Indonesia. Australia's closest large neighbour is our most promising potential strategic partner because of its size and location. Its proximity means its strategic interests are more likely to converge with ours, because a threat to one increases the risk for the other. Its economic potential means it might be able to wield real strategic weight. And its closeness, combined with its maritime geography, means Australia could offer it substantial military help, giving Indonesia clear incentives to support Australia in return.

The aim should not be to build a treaty alliance. In fact, the model of alliances we have inherited from the Cold War – long-term, stable, all-encompassing, like ANZUS and NATO – will be of little use in preparing Australia for the changes unfolding in Asia. Relationships should be looser and more fluid, more like the temporary alignments between European powers in the turbulent power politics of the seventeenth and eighteenth centuries. In the new power politics of the Asian Century, such relationships could offer Australia substantial diplomatic and even military support when interests and objectives align.

Realising this potential with Indonesia will require a lot of work. It should therefore be a prime focus of Australia's strategic diplomacy. Expectations should be modest: Jakarta is a long way from being ready or able to contribute to the security of its neighbours and remains deeply committed to the Cold War ideal of non-alignment. But Canberra could lay the groundwork for future cooperation and mutual support by starting a frank, serious and private conversation with Indonesian leaders about the strategic challenges both countries face over the decades ahead. Nothing like that seems to have happened so far.

Third, Australia should be rethinking its military strategy and defence budget to create forces that can both defend Australia independently from a power such as China and provide real support to potential strategic partners such as Indonesia. Geography has done us a critical favour here. Like Australia, all our close neighbours are island nations, and their defence, like ours, depends on maritime forces; more specifically, on maritime denial – the capacity to deny hostile air and sea approaches. The capabilities we should build to achieve maritime denial in our own defence would allow us to make a major contribution to defending the islands to our north as well.

For example, the large submarine fleet required to defend the continent – twenty-four or thirty-two boats, rather than the twelve now planned – could provide a major contribution to the defence of Indonesia. A force this size would be achievable and affordable if the government's ill-conceived plans for a large surface fleet were abandoned, and the deeply troubled submarine program were overhauled. Only with such forces can Australia build meaningful and effective alliances with our neighbours. So self-reliance comes first.

But to do these things Australia's forces would need to be very differently configured, and much larger, than currently planned. So the imperative is clear. Australia cannot take the military backing of other countries for granted in the difficult years ahead. It needs to be able to stand alone, and to maximise the chances that it will find support from others. And this means it needs a much more radical rethink of defence planning than anything yet contemplated in Canberra. ∎

BALANCING ACT

Making sense of the Quad

Rory Medcalf

In this age of strategic contest, with China seeking to dominate a disrupted Indo-Pacific region, the challenge for Australia is to avoid conflict without compromising its interests and values. It can only succeed in this by working with others: when a nation's interests outweigh its capabilities, and the rising power's tactic is to isolate and intimidate, it must seek safety in numbers. The only realistic goal is competitive coexistence.

Until relatively recently, Australia and many other Indo-Pacific countries seeking security in the region were caught between the narrow choices of bilateralism and multilateralism. In the second half of the twentieth century, bilateralism dominated. The American-led alliance system in Asia was rigidly fixed to a "hub and spokes" model: America's friends and allies mediated their security relations through Washington, and had little to do with one another.

Then, as efforts to build regional cooperation gathered pace in the 1990s, there was an added overlay of a lowest-common-denominator multilateralism: optimistic dialogues where everyone was in, and nothing would happen until all agreed. What developed was an alphabet soup of high-sounding institutions, most impressively the ASEAN Regional Forum, or ARF, in which the A stood for the Association of Southeast Asian Nations, an acronym within an acronym. The result was more gruel than feast, marked by sustained failure to manage – let alone resolve – disputes between China and other claimants in the South China Sea.

No wonder the diplomatic trend of the times is a third way, in which countries find "like-minded" partners and band together in small groups. These are neither formal alliances nor ponderous multilateral organisations, but creative coalitions defined by convergences of interests, values and capabilities, and a readiness to work together, making them islands of relative trust and cooperation in a sea of troubles.

The new shorthand for this is "minilateralism", and the most prominent example is the Quad, short for Quadrilateral Security Dialogue. This forum has attracted much attention in Asia and beyond. Yet it is mired in controversy and myth.

The one thing clear about the Quad is who's in. The four sides to this diplomatic polygon are Australia, Japan, India and the United States. In theory, at least, it is a potent combination. These are, respectively, the world's fourteenth, third, fifth and single largest economies, and the thirteenth, ninth, third and single largest military spenders. Their officials and ministers are increasingly seen in the same room or on the same stage together – even if of late that stage has usually been virtual. Their agenda keeps expanding, and now spans maritime security, defence, infrastructure, investment, technology, cyber affairs, supply chains and public health. In all of these discussions, the context is increasingly China and its affronts to sovereignty and the rules-based order.

Beyond that, much is in the eye of the beholder. Some detractors conjure nothing less than an Asian NATO, an armed bloc that through its very existence will goad China to conflict. (Never mind that much of China's new coerciveness evolved during the decade 2007–2017, when the Quad was disbanded.) Advocates see its promise precisely in the potential to deter Chinese "adventurism". In a world where Beijing's propaganda bureaus project China's inevitable dominance, it could bring a degree of balance. After all, its members' collective defence budgets, populations and economies vastly outsize China's, and this will continue, whatever setbacks COVID-19 brings. Yet some critics decry this as false hope, arguing there is little point in aggregating the heft of four nations unwilling to share one another's sacrifices – a pseudo-league whose bonds will dissolve when the shooting starts.

It's all rather confusing. Few diplomatic gatherings have been so prone to exaggeration and misinterpretation.

These are still early days in the life of the Quad. So far it is more a safe space for sharing concerns about China than a phalanx of security guarantees against it. The Quad has mattered more for what it signifies than what it does. It stands for certain principles: nations' rights to choose their allies and partners, rather than be coerced by a would-be dominant power; the search for solidarity across national borders; and the support of a rules-based order.

Given its infancy, the future of the Quad remains malleable. The departure of Japanese prime minister Shinzō Abe, long its biggest champion, will test its staying power. Yet the more China rails against the Quad while coercing individual nations, the more its rationale for existence holds. As respected Indian analyst Tanvi Madan puts it: "If Beijing is wondering why the countries feel a quad might be necessary, it might want to look in the mirror."

The Quad has mattered more for what it signifies than what it does

To make sense of the Quad – its promise and limitations, and what it means for Australia – we must understand its origins.

Crisis as catalyst

The strange thing about minilateral groupings such as the Quad is not that they are happening but that they took so long. Isn't it normal for nations to choose their friends? In 2020, the COVID-19 pandemic is driving countries to reappraise friendships, seeking safety and solidarity in new, creative coalitions more than ever before. It has seen a

"Quad-plus" dialogue, in which the four key members were joined by Vietnam, South Korea and New Zealand, three Indo-Pacific nations whose public health response has proven in every sense salutary. So the COVID-19 shock may strengthen the Quad as a forum for wider cooperation.

This is fitting, since another cross-border catastrophe was where it all began.

On Boxing Day 2004, a massive earthquake occurred at the northern tip of Sumatra. It sent tsunami waves east and west. In total, more than 230,000 people were killed, more than half in Indonesia but some as far away as South Africa. Four countries – the United States, Japan, India and Australia – rapidly mobilised military assets for a coordinated effort at disaster relief, concentrating their assistance on Indonesia, Sri Lanka and Thailand.

It was a novel coalition of first responders, breaking down preconceived ideas of "Western" or "Asian". If the four had a shared geography, it spanned two oceans, just as the tsunami itself confounded rigid regional divisions such as East Asia, South Asia, Australasia and the Asia-Pacific. But this core group was bound by more than some emerging geopolitical consciousness of the Indo-Pacific: they all shared an interest in a stable maritime region, and had capabilities close at hand and a willingness to help. Their contribution was immense: Australia alone provided a billion dollars to support Indonesia's recovery.

Of course, there is no pure altruism in international relations, and this humanitarian operation had a complex backdrop. In those years after 9/11, America, confronted by terrorism, consumed by its Iraq misadventure and conscious that a strengthening China would bring risk as well as opportunity, was thinking afresh about its partnerships. It was cultivating a rising India after decades of estrangement. Japan was normalising as a strategic power after half a century of abnegation. Australia was seeking practical ways to engage with the region, balancing the US alliance and the unrealities of ASEAN diplomacy with a new self-confidence defined by its stabilising interventions in Timor-Leste and the South Pacific.

The original incarnation of the Quad was never purely about China. Indeed, all four participant nations were individually trying to build constructive ties with Beijing. This was a time of high and hopeful globalisation. US admirals imagined a "thousand-ship navy" involving all countries, including China, keeping the sea lanes open for trade and ocean resources stewarded for the common good. If there was a political message among this group, it was less about China and more about demonstrating to a predominantly Muslim Indonesia that, whatever the divisions of the so-called war on terror, America and friends were here to help.

Yet there was another strategic message, intended or not. Four unlikely and capable friends – four maritime democracies – had assisted a region in need, where a rising China had failed to deliver. Moreover, they had marshalled their navies around a zone of acute security interest to China: the Bay of Bengal and Malacca Strait. This was a highway for Beijing's burgeoning lifeline of oil imports.

Navies could one day apply the teamwork learnt in delivering aid to enforcing blockade.

Or so China feared. This became apparent in May 2007, when the four met to discuss the lessons learned from their humanitarian cooperation. Maybe they also shared a few words about the changing regional balance of power. But they can't have said much: the Quad talks consisted of four mid-level officials meeting briefly on the sidelines of an ASEAN Regional Forum conference in Manila. It should have been no big deal. Instead, Beijing saw a phantom menace, and soon went into diplomatic hyperdrive.

One reason was the timing of the Manila dialogue, just a few months before a multi-nation naval exercise. India and America had long held modest annual naval drills, called Malabar. These expanded in ambition as US–India ties strengthened, so that in 2007 Malabar was held twice and with special guests. First, Indian, American and Japanese forces combined in the Pacific. Then a second round brought in warships from Australia and Singapore, the five navies converging in the Bay of Bengal.

China reacted with public outrage and diplomatic protests. Its officials and media portrayed a plot to forge an "Asian NATO". The reality was very different. The exercise had been a one-off. Commitment to the dialogue was fragile.

Enter Australia's new Labor government in late 2007 under Kevin Rudd. Diplomatic folklore blames him, not quite fairly, for the demise of Quad 1.0. It is true that Rudd's foreign minister, Stephen

Smith, indicated in response to a journalist's question that their government was not planning a second round of talks – while standing beside his visiting Chinese counterpart. This was an awkward look. But it also gave Japan and India a scapegoat for their own growing reluctance. Japan's attachment had weakened after Prime Minister Abe suddenly left office in ill health. Indian ambivalence grew as its coalition government was disrupted by leftist parties rejecting truck with America. For Prime Minister Manmohan Singh, preserving the US–India civil nuclear deal was the priority. The Quad was expendable.

Australia, Japan and India [have] sought to shore up their ties with Washington

China prompts the Quad to regroup

The main criticism of the Quad back then was that it would needlessly provoke China down a perilous path of military modernisation and destabilising behaviour. Yet Beijing chose such a road anyway. The perils the Quad's critics thought it would invoke ended up arising in its absence. The next decade brought such geopolitical instability that the four governments became convinced their disbanded dialogue had been an idea ahead of its time.

The narrative is depressingly familiar now. In 2008, the global financial crisis emboldened China to abandon its decades of restraint. From 2012, the regime of Xi Jinping prioritised a strategy of relentlessly pursuing greatness: expansive assertiveness and uncompromising nationalism abroad, combined with extreme authoritarian control at home. Chinese paramilitary forces confronted Vietnam, the Philippines and Japan in disputed seas.

As Japan held firm, China shifted to the passive aggression of manufacturing and fortifying islands in the South China Sea, in violation of international law. Fears grew of escalation, even war. America pivoted to join allies and partners in pushing back, but not always convincingly. The Obama administration secured undertakings from Xi that rampant cybertheft would cease and artificial islands not be militarised. The flagrant breach of such promises underscored the failure of engagement, while waking America to the extent and nature of the China challenge.

In Tokyo, Abe's return to office in 2012 led to an assertion of Japan's strategic normality and pushback against China. High on this agenda was the cultivation of ties with India and Australia, plus a strengthening of the US alliance. In 2013, Australia recognised new realities, with a defence white paper redefining the region as the Indo-Pacific – a two-ocean system in which China's push into the Indian Ocean was of growing concern.

That same year, Beijing redefined the region in its own terms, as One Belt and One Road (later rebranded the Belt and Road Initiative): a vastness of land and sea across which it planned infrastructure, investment – and influence. Whatever the label, China's strategic presence was extended across the Indo-Pacific. After all, the "road" in Belt and Road was short for the Maritime Silk Road: the ports and sea lanes across the Indian Ocean to Africa and the Middle East, with a branch line into the South Pacific.

In the Indian Ocean, the People's Liberation Army Navy arrived in 2009 to counter piracy, and never left. Hopes receded for a cooperative future with India. Xi's meeting with new Indian prime minister Narendra Modi in 2014 was clouded by China's military incursions across the disputed mountain border, its submarines in the Indian Ocean and its growing strategic ties with India's rival Pakistan. By the time of a military stand-off in the Himalayas in 2017 – prelude to the brutal clash of June 2020 – the Modi government was grimly aware that the relationship of respect Xi wanted was categorically one-way.

For its part, Australia was discovering that hazard loomed at least as large as opportunity in relations with the new China. Intelligence agencies reported to government – and journalists to the public – that the nation's largest trading partner was conducting interference, through influence and espionage, using all means from cyber to people to money. Strategic risks that had seemed confined to Asian waters now manifested close by, in the South Pacific. And objecting to such developments prompted diplomatic pressure and economic coercion.

Globally, great-power competition was back. Then, in November 2016, America's struggling credibility in Asia was compounded by Trump's destabilising dysfunctionality. Australia, Japan and India, along with Washington's other regional allies and partners, now found themselves hedging between a revisionist China and an unpredictable

America. They sought to shore up their ties with Washington, while taking out the insurance of strengthening cross-bracing bonds with one another and looking more seriously to their own defences.

Yet the Trump administration was rattling China, too. For all its narrow nationalism and capricious anti-diplomacy, America was giving China pause, and on this at least there was bipartisanship in Washington. A national security strategy warned of comprehensive strategic competition with Beijing, and envisaged contesting Chinese dominance of the Indo-Pacific.

In November 2017, the Quad reconvened at last. But this was as much an act of American followership as leadership. Japan had been extolling a "democratic security diamond" for years, and Australia and India were now more than ready. Bit by bit, they had used the Quad's fallow decade to weave a wider security web: some strands with America, some without. Australia and Japan had intensified their US alliances, but other security relations had rapidly solidified: the United States and India, Japan and Australia, Japan and India, Australia and India.

Defensive triangles had formed, too: intelligence sharing and complex military exercises among Australia, the United States and Japan were augmented by trusted trilateral dialogues. A Quad by stealth had already emerged through these intersecting triangles. Australia, Japan and India conferred on how to engage with and temper the influence of Trump's America. Meanwhile, America, India and Japan had kept their own conversation alive, with the Malabar naval exercises now permanently including Japan, and Australia patiently pressing to be invited back in. The old Quad had served as a lightning rod for much of China's ire, but beneath its cover the maritime democracies had found themselves aligning all along.

The Quad is here to stay

Not even the Quad's most ardent advocates pretend it is the sole solution to Australia's strategic problem of navigating a contested Indo-Pacific. Rather, it is considered one part of a layered diplomacy model that includes elements of bilateralism, multilateralism and practical minilateralism. No nation is putting all its hope in the four-sided basket.

> **The Quad is not the only emerging alignment that counts**

The regional security dynamic is now largely about balancing against China's power, and this has both domestic and foreign policy consequences. Almost every significant nation is looking to its defences, even if the economic damage of COVID-19 demands doing more with less. For instance, Australia has undertaken to increase its military capability investments by 40 per cent, to $270 billion, over the next decade, with plans to acquire longer-range maritime strike weapons and a sovereign constellation of satellites to aid communications and targeting. This will make it more self-reliant in some areas of combat, but Australia will still be dependent on the United States for the levels of technology and intelligence required for sustained and intensive warfare.

In external balancing, the Quad has firmed up further since 2017. Ministers meet to coordinate policy from the top. Experts share sensitive assessments on the new horizon of risk, linking technology, economics, disinformation, disease and military security. Another fully fledged quadrilateral naval exercise has not yet eventuated. But two simultaneous manoeuvres in mid-2020 had the same effect, with one US aircraft carrier practising with Australian and Japanese forces in the Philippine Sea and another joining the Indian fleet in the Bay of Bengal.

This is also a reminder that the Quad is not the only emerging alignment that counts. There is also an imperative to reach beyond the obvious four, and canvass concerns broader than how to manage China. An Australia–India–Indonesia dialogue has been established, and could usefully tackle a large agenda, from irregular migration and illegal fishing to counterterrorism and social cohesion. Australia, France and India have collaborated successfully in search-and-rescue operations in the Indian Ocean, where between them they have a comprehensive picture of maritime traffic and environmental risk. These nations now make another useful trilateral group, whose foreign secretaries convened virtually in September 2020 to discuss everything from geostrategic concerns to the pandemic and protection of the ocean commons. France and Australia are already part of a less famous quadrilateral for diplomatic coordination in the South

Pacific, with America and New Zealand – a group that could become more active in helping smaller states prevent China from translating aid and investment into unchallenged political influence.

There is a new global dimension too, which may overshadow the Quad and much else besides. Pandemic travel restrictions are eroding the importance of geography in choosing friends – after all, when every diplomatic dialogue is just a video conference away, friendships can form across the world.

This year's ferment of diplomacy includes such ideas as a G7 expansion, to include Australia, India and South Korea; a "D10" of leading global democracies; and a strengthening of the Anglosphere Five Eyes alliance from intelligence-sharing into a full geoeconomic coalition.

And, despite some accusations to the contrary, Australia and the other middle powers have not abandoned dialogue or cooperation with Beijing. As I conclude in my recent book *Contest for the Indo-Pacific*, the Quad and all the other threads of the new security web are not meant as substitutes for talking to China, but rather to provide more confidence when doing so: ensuring that the terms of engagement are mutual and fair.

Still, plenty of questions remain about the Quad. As the full impact of COVID-19 emerges, will Australia's new partners really be able to sustain or build the strategic and economic weight we need them to? How durable is their political will? How should the Quad engage other partners, from Asia and beyond? Will its real legacy be as a transition arrangement, creating tolerance for other minilaterals, some yet to emerge? In the end, how do any of these blocs engage with Beijing and its own efforts to shape and invent institutions?

The Quad is almost certainly here to stay, having outgrown any particular configuration of political champions. It now commands broad political support in all four countries. Abe's departure may slow progress, but his successor will almost certainly stay the course. Joe Biden has promised a united front of allies and partners to balance China, in a core pillar of his foreign policy, if he wins this November – and the Trump administration, for all its other mistakes, has got the Quad right. In India, long-term public anger over this year's border bloodshed means a new openness to any foreign partnership that resists China. In Australia, the Morrison government looks likely to stick around for another term, but in any case there is clear bilateral support for the Quad and the overall priority of balancing Chinese power.

An ambitious future agenda

Several futures are plausible. The Quad could lead to more inclusive arrangements, with the seven-nation coalition on pandemic response a sign of things to come. Or, if America stumbles grievously after the election, we could see more investment in middle-power coalitions without America. Or, in the unlikely event that Beijing rediscovers the art of diplomatic adaptation and pulls back on its assertiveness sooner rather than later, the Quad could matter less.

But the strategic anxieties and activist diplomacy of Quad

members in 2020 point a different way: to a strengthening of the Quad and an ambitious agenda.

On the defence front, it is almost certainly a matter of time before the Australian navy rejoins the Malabar exercises. In any case, maritime deterrence is now just part of a many-layered game. Joint military preparedness could be an increasing reality, involving training, technology sharing, intelligence exchanges and coordinated sea-lane surveillance. Forces may be granted access to and resupply at one another's bases.

Australia, India, Japan and America are also likely to find themselves cooperating far beyond the military domain. Australian diplomatic activism should focus on this broaden-

The Quad and its minilateral kin are not all about banding against China

ing of the Quad's mission, and ensuring that it reinforces the efforts the four countries are already making in twos and threes. For instance, the Quad and the Australia–Japan–India triangle can build diversified and resilient supply chains in vital areas such as medical equipment and the processed rare earths essential for advanced technologies. As the cyber and information realms become permanent battlegrounds, the four nations may try to align in setting standards and principles for cybersecurity, telecommunications and critical technologies related to the Internet of Things, the computer-to-computer data transfer that now pervades daily life.

Quad members could also coordinate on aid and infrastructure funding, ensuring that their resources – however frugal – are deployed more effectively to temper the influence and mitigate the risks of Beijing's Belt and Road Initiative. Likewise, the Quad can cooperate on so-called "capacity-building": providing assistance and training to smaller or developing countries in everything from maritime patrolling to the bolstering of democratic institutions (and yes, this will be more credible and effective if America gets better at safeguarding its own). We may also expect to see Quad countries coordinate more openly as a caucus to shape the debate in larger institutions, from the East Asia Summit to global forums.

There is plenty of work ahead for the Quad and other minilaterals without the need for firm alliances, complete with treaties that trigger mutual obligations. Every time a Quad official notes publicly that Asia lacks a NATO, as US Deputy Secretary of State Stephen Biegun did in August 2020, headline writers claim to reveal a secret American ambition to harden the Quad that way. But even Biegun's public remarks inviting the region "at some point to formalise a structure like this" also referred to the more inclusive analogy of the European Union – and moreover stressed how difficult and unrealistic the multinational alliance option was any time soon. India, for one, will not easily shake off its long allergy to alliance entanglements.

Even so, in the event of a future strategic crisis, some alliance-like actions by the Quad are becoming conceivable. Mutual help need not mean frontline sacrifice. The violent clash with Chinese forces in the Galwan Valley this year reinforced public support for the Quad in India, even though its forces fought alone and expect to do so again.

Of course, the Indian navy is as unlikely to confront China around the Senkaku/Diaoyu Islands as Australian soldiers are to reinforce the Himalayan passes. The contest is more complex than that. On intelligence, logistics, technology and diplomatic support, Quad coordination in the future becomes more conceivable with each act of China's serial coercion. In a fast-changing world, it is even becoming imaginable that Quad countries may one day find themselves coordinating – in ways short of frontline combat – to oppose Chinese coercion directed elsewhere, such as against a South-East Asian country or Taiwan.

Yet in the end, the Quad and its minilateral kin are not all about banding against China. Indeed, some aspects of minilateralism may serve China's long-term interests, provided Beijing recognises that its safest future involves settling for something less than dominance.

Minilaterals without America show that middle players have agency too: not everything is about taking sides between two risk-prone giants. Some combination of, say, Australia, Japan, India, Indonesia and Vietnam would show regional powers collectively and authentically shaping their future – and the idea that such substantial nations could form a grouping of their own later this century is intriguing. As for the Quad or other minilaterals involving America, these are not about Washington imposing its worldview on reluctant partners. They can be vehicles for the other members to join forces to engage with and moderate their American ally, to help it meet the challenge of competitive coexistence, rather than vehicles for confrontation and conflict.

The Quad is neither a perilous entente that will provoke a 1914-style conflagration nor the miracle solution to the democratic world's angst about Beijing's power. Instead, it is just one variation on a minilateral theme likely to resound throughout the 2020s. And none of these minilaterals can substitute for robust national security, a sound bilateral alliance, patient multilateralism or prudent engagement with China. But, if handled carefully and realistically, minilaterals can complement each of those instruments, and that is the point. ■

BLIND SPOT

Why Australia needs a
South-East Asia step-up

Karen Middleton

As COVID-19 swept through Asia earlier this year, Australian officials made some calamitous calculations about the likely trajectory of infection. While the worst-case projections were grim for several nearby countries, particularly Papua New Guinea, for Indonesia they were catastrophic: by the end of 2020, a possible death toll in the millions. The social, economic and security implications were almost beyond comprehension. Yet there was no boost to Australia's aid budget to help address the threat.

In late July, four months after these projections, the government donated 100 ventilators as part of a $2 million coronavirus aid package to Indonesia for virus-related medical and laboratory equipment. The contribution was announced in a statement to the Indonesian media by Australia's ambassador to Jakarta, Gary Quinlan. Underlining its security dimensions and the straightened diplomatic and aid budgets, it was funded not through the Department of Foreign Affairs and Trade (DFAT) but through the Department of Home Affairs.

This is small beer. In the wake of both the 1997 Asian financial crisis and the 2004 Indonesian tsunami, Australian aid ran into the billions. Some foreign policy and development specialists argue that Australia's lack of substantial support for South-East Asia, particularly Indonesia, during the pandemic reflects a deeper, long-running failure to strengthen ties with countries across the region. Despite Australia's professed commitment to engage with its neighbours, many feel the reality doesn't match the rhetoric.

As the pandemic took hold, the government abandoned its first review of Australia's aid budget in nine years, on the basis that priorities and the capacity to deliver funding were in flux. Instead, it unveiled a two-year interim plan, Partnerships for Recovery, to deliver COVID-19 assistance to the Indo-Pacific. The bulk of the initial $280 million funding, announced on 29 May, went to the Pacific and Timor-Leste, reflecting the government's priorities as part of its "Pacific step-up" under Prime Minister Scott Morrison. The remainder was allocated to the rest of South-East Asia, including $21 million to Indonesia.

It may sound generous, but this investment consists of unspent funds from the 2019–20 period, redirected from scholarships, volunteering programs and other projects that could not be delivered due to the pandemic. Given that those restrictions will prevail for some time, it is safe to assume this won't be the last reallocation of funds.

Months later, and with the regional death toll still climbing steeply, there is no indication of any significant new spending. This is not merely due to Australia's sudden domestic needs. Australian aid to South-East Asia was being scaled back long before COVID-19. In the five years to 2019–20, the government cut official development assistance to South-East Asia by 30 per cent, and to Indonesia by 50 per cent.

In early March, shadow foreign affairs minister Penny Wong raised the cuts with DFAT officials during a senate budget estimates hearing. "Surely it would be a good thing for the relationship if we didn't reduce our development assistance to them at a time when we want stronger ties with the region?" she asked.

Early plans for the international development policy were "essentially completely Pacific focused"

DFAT secretary Frances Adamson responded by highlighting the changing needs of Australia's aid partners: "Of course, it goes to relative priorities."

Australian officials note, not unreasonably, that coronavirus adds a layer of wicked complexity to aid delivery. The attitude of neighbouring governments is also relevant: Indonesian ministers have faced criticism for taking a denialist stance on the virus. Officials point out that they can't easily provide what is not wanted.

Australia's overall aid budget is currently $4 billion – the same level it has been at for five years. In 2014, foreign minister Julie Bishop announced that the annual aid budget, then $5 billion, would rise each year in line with the consumer price index. Instead, it fell by $1 billion in 2015's midyear budget update – a cut to fund "budget repair" and "policy priorities" – and has stayed there ever since.

Now the government is cutting personnel, too, including in key South-East Asian posts Jakarta and Manila. In mid-July 2020, Adamson notified DFAT staff that due to another reduction in the department's budget, jobs would go. DFAT was again being asked to do more with less.

Some who attended consultations on the planned overhaul of the aid budget – before the pandemic halted the review process – claim that South-East Asia was barely to be included at all. Melissa Conley Tyler, a research fellow from the University of Melbourne's Asia Institute, said early plans for the international development policy were "essentially completely Pacific focused".

"And that would have been a real loss for Australia ... You just have to keep saying, 'And don't forget this other really important region to us, don't have narrow thinking, think about our interests across the region and the range of countries that are important to us.'"

The federal government acknowledges that the nations of South-East Asia are hugely important to Australia. It's in all the official documents – the 2016 Defence White Paper, the 2017 Foreign Policy White Paper and this year's strategic and COVID-linked international development updates. But there is growing concern among analysts in the region that the aid cuts reflect a wider diversion of Australia's attention from South-East Asia. In expanding their Indo-Pacific focus to the west and east over the past decade, have successive Australian governments gradually lost sight of the middle?

Allan Gyngell, president of the Australian Institute of International Affairs, says, "We just can't wish a relationship with our closest neighbours away. But if you look at the aid budget, you can see that is the direction we've been going. They have been arguing that these are wealthy countries now which don't need our aid, so we are going to give more to the South Pacific."

Gyngell describes the lack of focus on South-East Asia as an "absence that needs to be addressed", just as the government is now fostering relations with India and Japan and pursuing more active engagement with Vietnam. "But it's harder to think of ways in which they have imaginatively tried to engage South-East Asian countries in new ways. And I think that's just partly because it is damn hard. It really is hard work. It requires an awful lot of commitment by ministers and prime ministers to keep turning up there."

Australia's unfinished business

Since 2013, Australia has replaced the term "Asia-Pacific" with "Indo-Pacific" to reflect a broadening of its region of strategic interest. This redefinition was the work of former foreign and defence minister Stephen Smith and senior official Peter Varghese, the former DFAT secretary, Office of National Assessments chief and high commissioner to India. Their approach was founded in economics, but factored in security implications in case, as Smith puts it, "China went bad".

The concept of the Indo-Pacific had already been floated in India and Japan. A proliferation of trade and security groupings had emerged, but there was a lack of consensus on how best to define the region for the purposes of encouraging cooperation. Proposed changes in security and economic architecture had to reflect the fierce independence that grew from the region's colonial past. Even the language required great care.

Prime Minister Kevin Rudd had previously sparked controversy in June 2008 with his proposal for an "Asia-Pacific community", unveiling it in a speech without running it by the neighbours. Rudd outlined his objective to US secretary of state Hillary Clinton during a meeting in Washington in March 2009, as revealed in a cable summary published by WikiLeaks in 2010. He explained his proposal was aimed at mitigating China's influence at the East Asia Summit and ensuring there was not "an Asia without the United States".

At that stage, the East Asia Summit involved China but not the United States. The Asia-Pacific Economic Cooperation group – which was determinedly about trade and not security – excluded India. The leaked cable revealed Rudd's Asia-Pacific community was envisioned to "fulfil a role similar to the Helsinki Commission in Europe, focusing at least initially on low-level common security policy and coordination, perhaps starting with humanitarian assistance and disaster relief". It was to have commenced in 2020.

The response was mixed, at best. Former prime ministers Bob Hawke and Paul Keating queried the value of trying to emulate

Europe, and officials and analysts in Indonesia, Malaysia and Japan expressed reservations.

The "Indo-Pacific" concept, which the Trump administration has now also embraced, is often seen as a vehicle for balancing the growing regional weight of China, just as Rudd's Asia-Pacific community was designed to be. But its origins were officially economic rather than geopolitical.

The analysis went that since World War II, Australia's direct foreign investment had been mainly in Britain, the United States, the European Union and Japan. Its major trading partners in North-East Asia, through iron ore, coal and eventually liquid natural gas, were Japan, Korea

Coronavirus [has] only underlined the need for Australia to build closer trade and economic ties in the region

and China. But Smith and Varghese assessed that most middle-class spending growth would come from India and South-East Asia – primarily Indonesia – and that by mid-century, the world's top four economies would be China, India, the United States and Indonesia, in that order.

Smith, now a professor of international law at the University of Western Australia and a board member of think tank the Perth USAsia Centre, argues that Australia's economic engagement with both India and Indonesia remains "substantially underdone". "We [wanted] them to be looking south to Australia, not just north to

North-East Asia, Europe and North America," he said in an interview in July 2020. "And so we started using the phrase 'the Indo-Pacific', and started having conversations with the strategic notion of the Indo-Pacific with India, with the United States, with Indonesia and with ASEAN."

The coronavirus pandemic's interruption to supply chains and escalating US–China tensions have only underlined the need for Australia to build closer trade and economic ties in the region. Australian business is still deeply invested in China, far more than in the broader Asian region. It now faces calls to diversify at a time of great stress.

Yet neither the shift of focus to the Indo-Pacific nor Australia's long period of uninterrupted economic growth – from 1991 to 2020 – has made business much more inclined to expand into South-East Asia, given the effort required. Both the government and the nation's business community will need to be involved in changing this pattern.

The optimists point to the free trade deal between Indonesia and Australia, the Indonesian Australian Comprehensive Economic Partnership Agreement, which took effect on 5 July 2020, stripping tariffs from Indonesian imports and broadening access to Indonesian markets for Australian goods.

But an interim report on Australian business prospects in Asia, published in July 2020 by the Business Council of Australia and the Asia Society's Asia Taskforce, confirms that in 2019 Australian business invested more in New Zealand – a country of five million people – than in the entire Asian region, home to almost five billion.

It found that while investments in ASEAN countries had increased by $32 billion over the past twelve years, this still only totalled $45 billion in 2019, almost half of which was invested in Singapore.

The report acknowledged the difficulties of doing business in parts of the region. Governance issues, red tape and corruption are all impediments. But it emphasised both Australia's opportunity and its responsibility to help lift living standards there:

> As one of the few developed economies in our region, we are well placed to help other countries prosper in the coming decades. A prosperous Asia will be good for the region's people but it is also good for our economic and security interests . . . We may have been handed a second chance by COVID-19 to lift our economic engagement with Asia. We should not waste it.

So far, the pandemic has sent things in the opposite direction. Australian banks and other service deliverers have begun shifting their offshore call centres back home. Westpac confirmed it was axing 1000 jobs in India and the Philippines and returning them to Australia. It is good news for Australian employment and for those frustrated by speaking to an operator without local familiarity, but bad news for regional support and engagement, and it will do little to address the analysts' concerns. Like industry, Australian governments have arguably been taking the easy road in avoiding forging stronger links in South-East Asia. They have looked first to their Five Eyes partners, the core of Australia's intelligence and security relationships and fellow members of a democracy club which all also happen to have English as a first language. But the rise of China under Xi Jinping has reinforced the need to re-engage with South-East Asian nations, which are watching the rivalry between Beijing and Washington with varying degrees of alarm.

As Asia Society senior fellow and former DFAT deputy secretary Richard Maude, author of the 2017 Foreign Policy White Paper, observes: "Quietly, behind the scenes, they're looking for partners to do things with and I think they're interested in what Australia has to offer ... COVID-19 has come on the top of that and they're interested more than ever in our help as well."

China's current aggression illustrates that upheavals in the rules-based order and other crises in international affairs have not been suspended while everyone washes their hands and drains their coffers. Countries in the region looking for help are turning to China, which is willing to take advantage of the instability. Philippines president Rodrigo Duterte has appealed to Beijing to help his country jump the queue for any vaccine, an offer China is making to a number of regional nations. Duterte has also failed to press China to abide by international law on the South China Sea.

As the health crisis worsens, the imperative to strengthen relationships and anticipate, mitigate and manage the looming challenges becomes greater, not less. Those relationships require persistent and patient work over a long period. As former prime minister John

Howard was fond of saying, "You can't fatten the pig on market day." Have we done enough of it? Are we doing enough now?

On the face of it, the answer is no.

Talking to the neighbours

In February 2020, just a month before those COVID-19 projections were made, Indonesian president Joko Widodo addressed Australia's parliament and called his host country "Indonesia's closest friend". Typically, though, neither country much mentions the other with depth or regularity.

Former Indonesian vice-presidential adviser Dewi Fortuna Anwar observes that, as a democracy, Indonesia is "not that different from Australia" – noisy and featuring sometimes acrimonious and contested decision-making: "This is a modern society, very outward-looking despite all of the challenges we face. That has not really filtered very much to the awareness of the Australian public. When they look at Indonesia, they either still see it as being military dominated [or] very extremist Islamist, where terrorists run round with impunity."

Australia regularly undermines its own reputation as a straight shooter

The 2020 annual Lowy Institute poll confirms the level of public ignorance in Australia about Indonesia, with only 39 per cent of respondents aware that it is a democracy.

But Indonesia doesn't pay huge attention to us either, Anwar confirms. "In a way, this is an asymmetrical [relationship] where quite often Australia pays more attention to Indonesia and where Indonesia becomes a domestic political issue in Australia ... while Australia, I would argue, never enters into Indonesian domestic political discourse."

John Blaxland, professor of international security and intelligence studies at the Australian National University, says that Jakarta respects Canberra, but Australia should not expect much public praise inside Indonesia other than on ceremonial occasions. "No self-respecting leading Indonesian politician is going to go out on a limb talking about how good Australia is, but behind closed doors they will happily engage because they know what you see is what you get. We're not good at playing games. We don't wear masks."

Yet Australia regularly undermines its own reputation as a straight shooter. The government increasingly fails to telegraph its actions, even to its important regional partners. Most recently, Australia's call for an independent, international investigation into the origins of COVID-19 raised eyebrows due to Canberra's lack of consultation.

A senior analyst in the Australian Strategic Policy Institute's Defence and Strategy Program, Huong Le Thu, says some in the region believed the call for an inquiry was too confrontational. But, she adds, "I've heard different [reactions] in private – 'Okay, it's good that someone has done that,' because they are not in the position to do it."

Kevin Rudd, now president of the Asia Society Policy Institute, believes that Australia should tread carefully when advancing diplomatic initiatives, such as the inquiry into the origins of COVID-19. "There was nothing wrong with the Australian government being party to calls for a global inquiry. But rather than do it unilaterally, bring ten governments along with you." Rudd knows well the consequences of non-consultation: while a key goal of his Asia-Pacific community eventually came to pass – the United States joined the East Asia Summit – it was not achieved without diplomatic stress.

Julie Bishop, now chancellor of the Australian National University, has also criticised the government's approach to the COVID-19 investigation. At the university's Crawford Leadership Forum in July 2020, Bishop said Australia should "ask for what it can get" and that there was "no way we could ever demand weapons-inspectors-level investigations without the backing of the [UN] Security Council", on which both China and Russia have veto powers.

> I would have called for an investigation, absolutely. I would have had like-minded countries backing it, if I felt it was something Australia had to lead … But if you wanted to actually achieve an investigation that enabled you to go into China and visit the Wuhan laboratories or anything else, you have to do it with China's cooperation. And the only way you're going to get that is talking to China behind the scenes.

Her comments suggest the government may have had ulterior motives. Rudd openly accuses Canberra of seeking to make domestic political capital out of the regional tensions with China. Dewi Fortuna Anwar does too.

Anwar also argues that Australia repeatedly fails to consider the regional consequences of decisions taken at home. She points to Australia's reflexive 2011 ban on exporting live cattle – introduced without warning – and, she says, more significantly, Canberra's sudden announcement during the 2018 Wentworth by-election that it would follow the United States in shifting its embassy in Israel from Tel Aviv to Jerusalem. The Gillard government's failure to make a courtesy phone call to Indonesia about plans to station US Marines in Darwin as part of President Barack Obama's "Pivot to Asia" was another point of contention with some in Indonesia. It fuelled conspiracy theories about an Australian agenda to facilitate Papuan independence. Anwar observes: "I mean, you told us that we are your partners. Partners talk to each other."

These faux pas are routinely dismissed in Canberra as inconsequential. The underlying relationships with key regional partners are certainly solid enough to withstand them. But they aren't helpful, either.

Increasingly, Australia has been sending mixed messages not only to Indonesia, but to the wider region. In the 2019 Lowy Lecture, Scott Morrison distanced Australia from multilateral institutions and condemned what he called "a new variant of globalism" that elevated them "above the authority of nation states". But by June 2020, after Australia had begun its advocacy for the COVID-19 investigation through the World Health Assembly, foreign minister Payne had shifted the tone: "Well-functioning global institutions lead to improved outcomes for the citizens of states that act cooperatively."

Likewise, there is a puzzling gap between rhetoric and action in the 2020 Defence Strategic Update. It was billed as a major boost to Australia's military to meet the greatest threat since the 1930s. Yet the actual commitment in new dollars and personnel is small. Other countries notice such anomalies.

Some are urging the government not to miss a diplomatic opportunity

Any upside Australia may find in being the outspoken member of a neighbourhood that is otherwise concerned with saving face lies in it being dependable and honest and matching word to deed.

A South-East Asia step-up

The COVID-19 crisis represents a chance for Australia to demonstrate its commitment to the region, beyond the prism of security concerns about China. As the pandemic continues, the government should publicly make the case that increasing support to South-East Asia will be for the stability and prosperity of us all. Instead, Australia's much more public focus is on its alliance with the United States and the growing tensions with China.

The United States let South-East Asia down during the 1997 Asian financial crisis, failing to join those assembling a rescue package and declining to bail out Thailand, one of only two countries in the region with formal US security ties. It cemented a view in Asia that Washington was driven by narrow, short-term interests.

In contrast, Australia contributed to the rescue package and was also there for Indonesia after the 2004 tsunami with a billion-dollar bailout. These things are not forgotten. They set Australia apart from the United States, at a time when regional powers are deeply uncertain about American reliability. As Australia is seen to increasingly follow Washington's lead, another generous offer of support might be a good thing. Some are urging the government not to miss a diplomatic opportunity.

Such a move would also serve to underscore the values we seek to uphold. The Morrison government is determined to voice its opposition to China's trade and security hostilities and cyber intrusions, and to resist pressure to change policies that China dislikes.

But the values argument becomes complicated as Australia grows closer to countries that are not open democracies. For instance, Canberra is finding its strategic relationship with Hanoi increasingly valuable. That Vietnam is a communist state with a questionable human rights record is somewhat inconvenient, diplomatically.

Richard Maude believes that Australia can balance this values equation successfully, continuing to criticise such countries even as it tries to draw closer to them:

> We're in an era where the geopolitics means we have to live – probably more than we would like to – with those inconsistencies and contradictions. But [that] doesn't mean we should let Vietnam off the hook. Or Indonesia or Malaysia or whoever it is … These relationships are robust enough now to withstand attention that comes from Australia making arguments to them about human rights, publicly and privately. In other words, we don't have to just say nothing or do nothing. And to be fair, DFAT still does do its best on human rights with these countries.

Marise Payne dismisses those who question the government's commitment to South-East Asia based on the level of official development assistance. She suggests that perceives the situation through a "simplistic and very narrow lens": "We work incredibly closely with our partner governments to ensure that what development assistance we provide is spent in line with their priorities, their national interests and in the interests of the region … These partnerships extend a long way these days, in 2020, beyond just our development funding."

Within the parameters of a shrinking aid budget, the government is searching for practical ways to help. Its assistance includes programs to assist neighbouring countries to manage welfare systems and the provision of economic and fiscal policy advice. It is also working with Gavi, the Vaccine Alliance – which established the global COVAX initiative for equitable vaccine access with the Coalition for Epidemic Preparedness Innovations. Their partnership is aimed at ensuring South-East Asian countries can access a COVID-19 vaccine – when one becomes available – at an affordable price.

The rules of bodies such as Gavi mean nations gradually lose access to concessions as their economies build. But Australia is taking the view that to exclude some with enormously vulnerable populations because their national gross domestic product tips over an arbitrary line would be patently counterproductive.

In July 2020, Payne and defence minister Linda Reynolds ran the coronavirus gauntlet to travel to the United States for the annual AUSMIN (Australia–United States Ministerial Consultations). They also met with Gavi representatives about finding ways around its rules on concessions. The AUSMIN talks resulted in a pledge to co-convene a second South-East Asia health security donor coordination meeting before 31 December and to jointly extend support for an existing three-year pandemic preparedness program through Palang Merah Indonesia, the Indonesian Red Cross. Payne has since also confirmed Australia is providing personal protective equipment and help with testing to Indonesia. In August, she announced $80 million for Gavi towards subsidising vaccine access for the Pacific and South-East Asia.

So things are happening. What is not is a public conversation, a seizing of the COVID-19 moment, to demonstrate the extent of Australia's commitment to the region and to remind Australians why spending on our neighbours, not just ourselves, is so vital to our national interests.

Allan Gyngell believes that aid is key to influencing emerging economies to see the world as Australia does. "China is having more influence in South-East Asia. It is clearly true that with Cambodia and Laos they've got close friends. But if we're not planning to leave the region to China, then we've got to be engaged ourselves in responses to that."

Australian government ministers argue, rightly, that their top priority must be domestic. But no minister thus far has been inclined to prosecute the argument, forcefully or otherwise, that funding a stable and secure Indonesia and South-East Asia is crucial to Australia's security, especially in the current context.

> **The nations of South-East Asia are sending a clear message ... "Do not make us choose"**

Had such a discussion started long ago, it might not need to go straight to those frightening pandemic figures. It is possible to talk up South-East Asian engagement in positive terms – the economic opportunities, the common geostrategic interests, the friendship. But it rarely happens, so here we are.

Meanwhile, as regional tensions increase, the nations of South-East Asia are sending a clear message to China, the United States and America's allies. They thrived on the status quo that prevailed before the great-power contest and desire neither conflict nor collusion. As Anwar puts it, "When elephants fight, grass suffers. But when they make love, grass also gets trampled."

ASEAN nations are issuing what is more a plea than a warning: "Do not make us choose." They want continued US engagement in the region but are preparing for the prospect of US withdrawal. That requires Australia to increase its diplomatic efforts and aid funding, not the reverse. As John Blaxland says, "We need to not only step up ourselves but work as closely as possible with all the like-mindeds we can find in the neighbourhood. All of them. Not just India, not just Japan – anybody who will reach out a hand of friendship."

The pandemic represents both a threat to regional stability and an opportunity to prove our bona fides through a substantial, dedicated neighbourhood response in the form of diplomacy and aid. Even if we can't shake hands just now, we can surely grasp that. ∎

GOODBYE, AMERICA

The remaking
of Asia

Patrick Lawrence

In March 2020, what the US Defense Department now calls its Indo-Pacific Command asked Congress for slightly more than US$20 billion to cover a six-year expansion of its operations across East Asia. Congress had invited the Pentagon's request, effectively saying, "You need more money. Ask and you shall receive." Few questioned this course.

This is all about China, to state the obvious. More to the point, it is about prolonging American primacy in the Pacific as the People's Republic emerges as a regional and global power. This is a forlorn project by any balanced reckoning. Yes, America will remain a Pacific power. No, it can no longer presume pre-eminence. The compulsion to insist otherwise arises out of longing for the once-was, anxiety in the face of change and an appallingly poor grasp of China's aspirations and intentions.

Admiral Phil Davidson, who heads the Pacific Command, cast his submission to Congress as part of a strategy he called Regain the Advantage. Somewhere along the line the United States lost the advantage, he wants us to know. Numerous members of Congress joined Davidson, invoking American "credibility" and speaking of "reassuring US allies and partners". We have been here before, of course. This is the same boilerplate one heard when the Soviet Union, warhead counts, "missile gaps" and all the rest were at issue during the Cold War decades.

The comparison is portentously apt. After years of low-wattage hostility, the United States committed to a new Cold War with China this past northern summer. This one is almost certain to remain cold by design: only fools imagine a hot conflict with the mainland could be won, and while there seem to be fools aplenty at the Pentagon, it is unlikely there are enough of them to carry the day on this point. But Cold War II will nonetheless prove as divisive and ruinously wasteful as the first. In the matter of friends, allies and enemies, Asians and their southerly neighbours will have some serious sorting to do.

Since Davidson's document landed on Capitol Hill, the House and Senate have been busy massaging the numbers to determine how much to spend on what they prefer to call the Pacific Deterrence Initiative. However these authorisations are allocated, the United States is about to buy a greatly enhanced, more visible military presence in the western Pacific. These outlays are very precisely marked – enlarged stockpiles of long-range weapons, air defence and radar systems, landing facilities for F-35A fighter jets, lots of money for military construction in cooperating nations. Davidson wrote of "projecting credible combat power at the time of crisis" when he asked for the funding Congress had asked him to ask for. His request included an "OPLAN" – a military operation plan ready for full-dress execution "if it becomes necessary". This is Cold War II made flesh.

The future arrives as we speak. In mid-April, the US Navy sent three warships (and Australia one) into the waters off Malaysia in response to an unarmed Chinese vessel conducting routine seismic surveys in the area. In early July, the Pentagon sent two carrier strike groups into the South China Sea in its latest and largest "freedom of navigation" tour –

The "postwar order" in Asia was a most undesirable disorder

this as the Chinese Navy conducted exercises nearby. Nothing came of these incidents, and nothing was supposed to: they were in the way of acting out, with something of spectacle about them.

Ten days later, on 13 July, Mike Pompeo, America's primitively Manichaean secretary of state, turned US policy sharply when he declared in a press statement that China's maritime claims in the South China Sea were "completely unlawful". This marked an abrupt departure from Washington's professed neutrality as to jurisdiction over contested waters; it was greeted in some quarters, not least the foreign pages of *The New York Times,* as opening the door to war with China on behalf of nations contesting Beijing's claims. Nothing will come of this, either. It was a somewhat extravagant display, as Pompeo is wont to offer us, but display it once again was.

What does America intend to achieve by way of events and declarations such as these, or from its emerging military posture? What can one read into this past season of heightened tensions, and what will proceed from it?

A display of power is the most obvious answer. Washington wishes Beijing to see these ostentatious manifestations of American military force and accept the security order at the western end of the Pacific as this has been for the past seven decades. It wishes the rest of East Asia and the good people of Australia and New Zealand to be comforted: yes, the Yanks are still here. Do not miss the nostalgia in America's ever-unaltered wishes. I have long taken nostalgia to be a form of depression, an inability or refusal to address things as they are. This is America's fundamental affliction in the twenty-first century, from which sprout its numerous errors in foreign policy. It declines to accept the realities of the new century, and so is no longer leading. At base, its purpose is to hold onto the past and avoid facing either the present or the future, leaving it indifferent (or opposed) to what an imaginatively managed new order in the Pacific can be. This is a perilous state.

China is determined to redress historic wrongs and reclaim a place in the region it long ago lost, but it is nostalgic for nothing. With perfect justification, it finds nothing beneficial or worthy in prolonging the US-led security order, however much this may have served Beijing's interests during the years it was implementing the Dengist economic reforms. The rest of the Pacific littoral is best advised to take note. Wisdom in the year 2020 lies in checking the clock for the correct time, even if the nation from which I write insists its hands have stopped.

Boutros Boutros-Ghali, the former secretary-general at the United Nations, concluded *Unvanquished*, his 1999 memoir, with the observation that diplomacy is for weak nations, the strong having no need of it. The thought remains pertinent, but I must offer a correction. His Excellency confused strength and power, and we mustn't any longer. Diplomacy is twenty-first century statecraft's defining technology. In an era when conquest is no longer feasible, desirable or acceptable, it is vastly more effective than carrier groups and preposterously expensive hardware that, in the end, display nothing so much as how ill-equipped my country is to meet the tasks of our time.

Let me finish the point this way. Sending that warship into Malaysian waters in April was the very wrongest thing Australia could have done. One, to tag along after the Americans in such an unbecoming fashion is to follow them into the wistful mists. Two, the Malaysians proved the adults in the room when they told the US Navy to be on its way: we intend to negotiate these sorts of things, they advised with typically Asian courtesy. The Americans affect not to notice this inconvenient but obvious cue. Never mind them: it is best to take it.

The foreign ministry in Kuala Lumpur has a more useful take on where the Asia-Pacific is headed than the world's most elaborately armed military.

Asia without the West

During my years as a correspondent in Asia, one learned to think of the Pacific superstructure as a bicycle wheel, hub and spokes. American diplomats were especially fond of the image. Asian nations had weak relations among themselves. All ties were bilateral, emanating outward from the masters of ceremony in Washington. This was fine, supposedly. It was how the United States established and maintained the postwar order across the Pacific – supposedly.

Immediately there is a question of nomenclature. Throughout the Cold War decades, Americans cultivated the habit of not looking too closely at their "postwar order". What would they find were they to look attentively and honestly?

There were a lot of unhappy nations in the region during this period. Three decades of military dictatorship in South Korea endured until Roh Tae-woo, the last of the generals, stepped aside in 1993. The Marcos regime in the Philippines (1965–86); the Thai generals and Lee Kuan Yew's Singapore (ongoing stories, these); Suharto in Indonesia (1967–98, the worst of the lot in my view); General Nguyễn Văn Thiêu in South Vietnam; and the Chiangs *père et fils* – Kai-shek and Ching-kuo – in Taiwan: all of these ruled over nations that appeared more or less orderly if viewed from afar.

The truth is that the "postwar order" in Asia was a most undesirable disorder. And it implied the permanent presence of the US military and ongoing support for dictatorial regimes. It was exogenous, if you like: beneath it lay incessant repression, corruption and political malfunction. It was sustained in the name of countering the "communist threat" as presented (again, supposedly) by China.

The only sustaining source of order in any society derives from within: it is endogenous. And this may or may not imply a democracy. Some years ago, Partha Chatterjee, the noted Bengali scholar, observed that political legitimacy in our time, especially in the non-West, flows less from participatory political processes than from an administration's capacity to deliver security, basic services (education, healthcare, clean water) and infrastructure, and altogether a measure of prosperity and wellbeing. I do not especially like this thought, given my fundamental assumptions about politics and government. But are my assumptions any more than the luxuries of someone raised and trained amid the wealth of the West?

Asia no longer makes the mistake that modernising means Westernising

There are implications here as we think about a post-postwar order in the Pacific. Asia has gradually undergone a profound change of consciousness since the Cold War's end. It no longer looks to the West for instruction in government and politics. It no longer makes the mistake that modernising means Westernising. We can use-fully term what we witness the re-Asianisation of Asia. It is where the future lies, but it is also a return, a going back, a reclamation of a buried selfhood.

Some years ago, while walking along the tree-lined esplanade aside the Singapore Cricket Club's *padang* (pitch), I came upon a monument commemorating the Indian National Army (INA) – a force of Indian nationalists allied with the Japanese to fight the British in South-East Asia. The original stone did not long endure: Subhas Chandra Bose, the INA's co-founder, laid it in July 1945, and Lord Mountbatten had it destroyed as soon as Singapore fell. Here's the remarkable thing: Singapore, that most Western-tilted of South-East Asian nations, reconstructed the original monument, complete with respectfully written plaques in several languages, in 1995. Aghast, I jotted down details of the monument in one of those pocket notebooks correspondents learn never to be without. It told me something I, like most Westerners, had never quite registered.

In Asia today, Partha Chatterjee's Asia, there is no dividing line separating China from the rest. One way to think of the American project is as an effort to etch such a division. But the ideological dis-tinctions the United States likes to dwell on do not count for much. Being Asian counts for much. Contemporary Asia does not entertain any serious anti-Western animus of Chandra Bose's sort. America has a lot of frontage on the Pacific lake, and no one – not even the Chinese – wishes this to be otherwise. But that peculiar monument to the INA, tucked quietly along a well-tended promenade, has something to say to Westerners. Re-Asianised Asia will be modern in its own way. It shows few signs of observing America's imposed accounting of who its friends, allies and enemies are. It has a different set of axes.

This is especially important for the Western-associated nations of the Pacific to understand. Australia and New Zealand have, since their founding, viewed their Western identities as central. For a long while their Pacific identity ran a distant second, as if their location were a geographic anomaly. While neither will ever be Asian, it seems time these two countries become who they are – which is to say Pacific nations first, Western as a matter of heritage. It is the Australian and New Zealand analogue to the rest of the region's re-Asianisation. I will not inflict "Pacificisation" on readers, but the cumbersome term is roughly my meaning here. Asia re-centres itself in itself, not around the United States or any other distant power. So must its southerly neighbours. The bicycle wheel analogy is of no further use. This is the starting point as the western end of the Pacific seeks an endogenous, post-postwar order of its own devising.

The follies of Sinophobia

East Asians, excepting the Chinese and Japanese, made unpractised diplomats during my years of to-ing and fro-ing among them. Most Asians had little need of diplomacy, as all matters of consequence were determined in Washington (as was emphatically the case with the Japanese, the *Gaimusho*'s high professional standard notwithstanding). Underdeveloped foreign ministries may seem unpromising places to begin a renovation of Pacific relations. But the building blocks of any sort of region-wide, inclusive order lie in the elaboration of bilateral ties based on shared interests and aspirations. Only when Asian nations know one another will regional organisations logically follow. The most encouraging cases are in North-East Asia, maybe because this is where cooperative ties are most needed. And China is intimately part of the equation.

There is now much talk about the Quadrilateral Security Dialogue, which draws together the United States, Japan, Australia and India in what is effectively – no, entirely – an alliance dedicated to some vague combination of containing or countering China. The Quad has been an on-again, mostly off-again affair since it was hatched during the George W. Bush administration. It is excellent that the Pacific region is in search of new partnerships, alliances, coalitions. But the Quad is entirely off-track. A couple of years ago, Wang Yi, the Chinese foreign minister, marked it down as "sea foam in the Pacific or Indian Ocean" that will "soon dissipate". The Pacific littoral will be much better off if events prove Wang right.

It is the Quad's very design we must count as its fatal flaw. US participation in the Quad is problematic, to put the point mildly: the notion that Washington would consider itself one among four equals is sheer illusion. The Americans are simply not ready to assume any such post-primacy position, or even to contemplate it. What is the logic in responding to the decline in US influence by building an organisation that rests on it? The Japanese are another defect in the design. It always pains me to note this, but those in power in Tokyo remain creatures of the 1945 defeat and promise merely to reproduce old habits of deference in a framework wherein it has no place. As to India: nonalignment is dead; long live nonalignment.

Mike Pompeo's State Department and the Pentagon are doing their best to poison Pacific waters, but Asians show no intention of partaking in what is becoming a paranoiac frenzy of Sinophobia. Their southerly neighbours are ill-advised to do any differently. An organisation dedicated to isolating China will end up isolating those that belong to it from the rest of Asia. Plainly and simply, the Pacific has no need of a NATO-like military alliance. Wrong technology, wrong time on the clock.

China seeks nothing more than a role in securing its neighbourhood

A sound appraisal of China – or reappraisal, as the case may be – is essential to a sturdy post-postwar order. The Chinese, from Xi Jinping to the remotest villager, bear a collective memory of their "century of humiliation", which they date to the Opium Wars. So is parity with the West, in symbol, gesture and practice, entirely beyond negotiation? China nurses no desire to send the United States back to the California coast and claim the Pacific as its own. Nor does Beijing have some kind of imperial design on the region: territorial dominion and unlawful interventions are outdated Western proclivities, and let us not project. Since the US–China rapprochement in 1972, Beijing has sought cooperative relations with others and has often supported multi-party efforts to resolve disputes. Chinese diplomacy has proven essential in the North Korea question and the Iran nuclear accord, among other cases.

As to the South China Sea, China seeks nothing more than a role in securing its neighbourhood. Would any other nation wish differently? Its jurisdictional claims are broad and intersect with those of others, certainly, but Pompeo's "completely unlawful" comment is ... completely irresponsible, given all claims await either adjudication or negotiation, and parties to these disputes signal they prefer the latter. China's claims to South China Sea jurisdictions come to six; are grounded in law and history, just as those of others; and were asserted years after Malaysia's three to five (depending on how one counts), the Philippines' nine and Vietnam's forty-eight. The Association of Southeast Asian Nations is attempting to negotiate a code of conduct with China, but this seems a poor fit as too few members have a stake in the issue. *Qui tenet teneat,* he who holds may go on holding, seems to be the tacitly accepted arrangement. Informality, fluidity and mutuality reign for the moment, an approach that is to my mind very Asian. I haven't noted any Malaysians, Filipinos, Vietnamese or Bruneians banging on the Pentagon's door asking for wandering warships to come their way. Nor does the Duterte government in Manila seem to take much interest in the 2016 award made by an arbitration tribunal, set up under the United Nations Convention on the Law of the Sea, which was critical of China's claims. But it is into this serviceable-for-now breach that the United States – a party to none of this, of course – intrudes. Its freedom-of-navigation argument is a cynical ruse, plain and simple: the sea lanes are secure, will remain so, and bear no relationship to the competing claims to maritime sovereignty.

Thank goodness Asians understand where their future lies and does not. China looms large, naturally, but they accept it as a great power to be traded and negotiated with, invested in and at a neighbourly peace with. There is Australia, on the other hand: how it proposes to take part in any sort of new Cold War against its largest trading partner without risking economic decimation is incomprehensible. I simply cannot understand the audience the nation's China hawks and Sinophobes command.

The Economist recently carried the cover line "Trade without Trust: How the West Should Do Business with China". This is cake-and-eat-it stuff, English muddle at its finest. "A new trade regime is needed that acknowledges China's nature," the newspaper asserts. Wow. It is China's nature that the Anglo-American sphere habitually declines to acknowledge. It is a matter of sheer self-interest that Australia get on with the business of acknowledging.

Towards a self-made Asia

The thought of an Asian-made regional order is not so new or abstract as one might assume. Cast back to 2006. Kim Jong-il pays a state visit to Beijing. Christopher Hill, the Bush administration's point man on North Korea, goes to Beijing shortly thereafter. The six-party talks on Pyongyang's nuclear programs have the United States, China, Japan, South Korea and Russia on one side of the table and North Korea on the other. The Chinese are the go-between at a delicate moment.

Hu Jintao, China's president at the time, had previously been reluctant to assume any kind of leadership role on North Korea. Suddenly the United States was ceding control of the six-party talks to the Chinese. In 2009, the talks gave way to a longstanding mutual mistrust between Pyongyang and Washington. But on those occasions when they appeared promising, a number of participants informally discussed institutionalising the format for use in other contexts. Japan's island disputes – the Kuriles with Russia, the Senkaku/Diaoyu with China – may have been candidates for this sort of resolution.

The episode has contemporary echoes. When he won the South Korean presidency in May 2017, Moon Jae-in immediately set about reviving Kim Dae-jung's noted "Sunshine Policy" – the South's efforts to build economic and political relations with the North. Within a year, Moon gave KDJ's policy remarkable substance. Working with Beijing, Moscow and Pyongyang, the South Korean reformist developed blueprints for integrating North Korea into a coherent North-East Asian economic hub. The maps, impressively detailed, showed three transport corridors running from South Korea through North Korea to north-eastern China and the Russian Far East. There were plans for rail lines connecting to the trans-Russian system all the way to Europe, a major gas pipeline and industrial centres located to maximise shared benefit. The intent was integration – as it is with Xi Jinping's Belt and Road Initiative. The underdeveloped would develop, and the South would at last have open connections to the Eurasian landmass. Kim Jong-un, Jong-il's son and successor, was listening.

The United States took no interest in this planning and negotiating: once again it had effectively ceded the initiative to Asian powers. Moon's efforts coincided roughly with Trump's one-to-ones with the North Korean leader, and these, too, were promising. But there is Trump and his seat-of-the-pants ideas to reduce American commitments and

Writing a new script in the Pacific story will be hardest for Japan and Australia

expenditures abroad, and there is the permanent state around him, which entertains no thought of such reductions. Pompeo and John Bolton, national security adviser at the time, sabotaged the Trump–Kim encounters at their second summit, in Hanoi early in 2019.

Moon's larger intent was – and remains – to build nothing less than a post-postwar order in North-East Asia. One applauds the endeavour. He has not put it in so many words, but he has come close, notably as he arms-folded refuses to oblige Trump's demand that Seoul pay more for the 20,000-odd US troops stationed on Korean soil. Moon's project is locally grown, endogenous, and in its collaborative approach we find the potential for the sorts of partnerships the Pacific region can form. And in this case – useful because unusually plain – we have an example of just how destructive Washington is willing to be as Asia re-Asianises and takes back its future. The South China Sea question is a straight-ahead variant of this phenomenon.

Australia's new allegiance

It was increasingly evident in the Cold War decades that the United States had a security policy across the Pacific but not much of a foreign policy. During my years in the region I began to consider whether Washington had ever returned to a peacetime posture after the Allied victory in 1945. As so often, the answer lay in the question.

Asians today are clear about favouring a shift from the military-first paradigm that has defined America's trans-Pacific presence. I may not want to bring Rodrigo Duterte home to meet Mother, but the Philippines president has actively promoted peaceable ties with China since taking office four years ago. Others, such as the Malaysians, speak with softer voices. Moon Jae-in is a further case: close ties with the United States are not at issue; the aspiration is for ties on different terms.

Writing a new script in the Pacific story will be hardest for Japan and Australia. These two nations, present at the creation of our "postwar order", remain heavily invested in it. Why? I don't think the answers are as clear as these nations' commitments suggest. Both stand to derive much from a new reading of their circumstances.

The Japanese have nursed a pronounced ambivalence about their place in the world throughout the modern era. In 1885, Yukichi Fukuzawa, a prominent Meiji-era intellectual, published an essay called "Datsu-A Ron" ("Goodbye, Asia"). In our time there have been numerous refinements on the thought. We have *datsu-A, nyū-Ō* (leaving Asia, joining the West) and *datsu-A, nyū-Bei* (leaving Asia, joining America). More recently: *nyū-A, datsu-Ō* (joining Asia, leaving the West), *nyū-A, nyu-Ō* (joining Asia and the West both) and *nyū-A, shin-Ō* (joining Asia and being friendly with the West). I find *zai-A, shin-Ō* (being Asian or "existing in Asia", being friendly with the West) the most curious: it is a considerable leap after more than a century of neurosis about the national identity. It is an ideal, not a policy, like all the others, but it suggests the potential for a new direction.

During my years in Tokyo, one of the premiers I most liked covering (and there were plenty to choose from) was an agile, forthright thinker named Yukio Hatoyama. Hatoyama was a Gaullist, in political terms the Japanese borrowed from the French after World War II. He was, by my reckoning, a *nyū-A, shin-Ō* man: let's join Asia and stay friendly, but measuredly so, with the West. "The security treaty between Japan and the United States is perfectly natural," he once told me, "but it is surely time for a more equal partnership." On another occasion he remarked, "We must not forget our identity as a nation located in East Asia." He spoke often of "an East Asian community".

As leader of the Democrats, a young opposition party, Hatoyama won a resounding victory over the long-governing Liberal Democrats in 2009. The central planks of his platform were a reappraised alliance with the United States and the closure of Marine Corps Air Station Futenma, a US base in Okinawa responsible for inexcusably many episodes of drunken assaults of local residents, rapes, hit-and-run accidents and so on.

Hatoyama was out in nine months, done in by the Tokyo establishment for the very positions that made him popular. His sin lay not in his thinking, but in bringing his thinking to the surface in Japanese politics. Gaullism remains a streak in the Japanese political weave, even among Liberal Democrats. Yasuhiro Nakasone, noted for his friendship with Ronald Reagan, was a Gaullist. So was Junichiro Koizumi, who was at times obsequious towards America but nonetheless summitted in Pyongyang in 2002 as the Bush Jnr administration watched in gritted-teeth silence. Shinzō Abe, who resigned as premier this year after eight years in office, was cut from the same cloth: eager for broader Pacific engagement but staying well within the "American security umbrella". We will see where post-Abe Japan goes. It is likely to prove in the same direction Abe came to favour as his term extended to make him Japan's longest-serving postwar prime minister.

It is its submerged but unstilled current of Gaullism that offers a sustainable re-Asianised future, in my view. I read this into Japan's unusually attenuated response to America's new Cold War against China. In June, just as Pompeo was beginning to huff and puff, Tokyo somewhat boldly cancelled plans to purchase a US missile defence system intended to protect Japan against potential threats from China and North Korea.

This is a fraught passage for Australians. But I do not see they will have any more choices than Japan. The relationship with Britain has been uncertain since the Gallipoli campaign in World War I, and Britain's inadequacies as a protector were clear in World War II. Allegiances shifted to the United States, the declared Pacific power. Now America's inadequacies are clear and Australia's allegiances must shift again – to Australia, if you will. US interests in the Pacific have never been congruent with anyone else's, including Australia's, and this reality now can be blurred or wished away only at cost.

How salutary for a nation to begin thinking for itself after leaving this to others for so long

Australians seem to be coming to terms with this. The national hand-wringing is evident even at a distance, but the conversation is an excellent sign of things to come. If there is any alternative to "existing in Asia" – just the phrase, for the distinction it allows from "being Asian" – I cannot think of it.

The Morrison government took an interesting tack in July, when announcing Canberra's response to Beijing's imposition of its new security law in Hong Kong. Australia followed other Western nations in extending visas and suspending its extradition treaty with Hong Kong, and got spattered with China's ire just as they did. But the government made a point of putting Australia's response in the larger frame of its search for tech talent. "Australia has a long history of attracting Hong Kong's best and brightest who have contributed significantly to our economic growth and job creation," the prime minister announced. Skilled workers from Hong Kong will "attract talent and companies to our nation in order to boost productivity and create further job opportunities for Australians". Acting Minister for Immigration Alan Tudge echoed Morrison:

> We'll be prioritising applicants from Hong Kong ... to target those particular individuals who are real job-multiplying people, who create businesses, who are entrepreneurs, who have that tech talent that the world is looking for, frankly ... There is so much talent in Hong Kong. There are great businesses in Hong Kong. And we know that many individuals now might be looking elsewhere. We want to make it attractive for that super talent to consider Australia.

It is a small matter and the circumstances poor, but it is nicely perpendicular to those White Australia policies that lingered into the 1970s. I read this as a modest sign of a new and wise direction in Canberra's foreign policies, towards a reappraisal of its circumstances as a Pacific nation – and, in the best outcome, its alliances. But for now Morrison's regional posture remains predicated on prolonged American primacy, and this suggests Australia risks an error Japan is well along in making. Premier Abe appeared to be enjoying himself as he deployed naval vessels in a wider arc around the region – they were present during the Americans' provocative exercise in July. If this is supposed to display Japan's greater independence, it is sheer delusion. It is merely a reinvestment in the post-"postwar order". One hopes Australians recognise the distinction here. I don't know the Japanese for this, but the Quad amounts to staying with America very late in America's day, keeping Asia at a detrimental distance.

Australia's case of nerves during this interim is perfectly understandable. But anxiety and anticipation are the dark and light sides of the same moon, and there is much eagerly to anticipate as Australia becomes more Pacific and less Western. How salutary for a nation to begin thinking for itself after leaving this to others for so long. What opportunities, what prospects for fruitful new partnerships lie ahead when it enters into a new order that is assuming shape as we speak – an order expressive of the interests and aspirations of those creating it, and no one else's. ∎

THE FIX

Solving Australia's foreign affairs challenges

—

Allan Behm on Why Australia Should Convene a Pacific Donors' Conference

"The countries of the Pacific want engagement . . .
But the leadership they seek involves cooperation,
dialogue, understanding and, above all, respect."

THE PROBLEM: International aid, or official development assistance (ODA), in the Pacific too often fails to meet its fundamental objective – a better life for Pacific peoples. Funding is in decline and, in a world shaken by COVID-19 and a massive global economic slump, it won't return to pre-pandemic levels quickly.

International spending in the Pacific also achieves far less than it should because many of the aid projects are unfocused and disconnected – both from one another and from long-term outcomes. Currently, there are more than 6000 projects underway in fourteen Pacific countries, funded by some forty countries and twenty specialised agencies. With so many players and poor infrastructure management skills in many of the recipient nations, the scope for confusion and waste is great. In April 2020, for instance, Papua New Guinea's High Commissioner to Australia, John Kali, slammed the nation's main aid donor, Australia, for what he described as "a loss of effective and transparent engagement".

The problem is compounded by the Morrison government's predilection for policy by slogan, rather than by good design. The government refers to the Pacific community as "our Pacific family", but the sentiment lacks substance. For example, the government insists on its commitment to the "Pacific step-up" despite withdrawing from the Green Climate Fund in 2018. Without that fund, Pacific island states have little chance of adapting to sea-level rises.

The Pacific step-up followed years of neglect and aid cuts, and is a thin disguise to contain China's influence in the region. The Sustainable Development Goals – the seventeen UN-mandated targets to address poverty, inequality, climate change, environmental degradation and injustice – have become a casualty of geopolitical rivalry. But Australia's plan is misguided: struggling Pacific countries, desperate for cash, will take grants and soft loans where they can.

Competition over ODA is counterproductive. Even if China's ODA activities in the Pacific are an attempt to bolster its political influence and power in the region, Australia and other key donors should engage with China, rather than risk seeming ineffectual and impotent.

Australia plans to spend $1.4 billion on ODA in the Pacific in 2019–20, which is more than the next four major donors combined, and almost five times the spend of China or the United States. As the largest donor to and neighbour of the recipients, Australia has much to benefit from ensuring that all international aid in the region is used effectively.

THE PROPOSAL: To ensure credible and effective development assistance in the Pacific, Australia should convene an annual conference for major ODA donors – both nations and organisations – and the Pacific nations that receive this aid.

This conference should be held across Pacific island capitals on a rotating basis, with Australia funding ODA recipients' attendance. While the Secretariat for the Pacific Community – a regional development organisation headquartered in New Caledonia – has attempted to go down this path, a 2016 Department of Foreign Affairs and Trade review found that it has yet to develop the financial management and programming skills to succeed.

The last thing the Pacific needs is another political talkfest, with gaudy shirts and floral coronets. This would be a forum for experts: it would bring together top ODA program administrators, designers and contractors from each major donor. Similar forums have been held elsewhere in the world – UN-backed donor conferences on Africa, for example, have been successful at coordinating aid programs, though they have been perhaps too numerous, and too narrow in their focus, to be as effective as they could be.

A Pacific conference could coordinate the delivery of aid programs and projects to ensure meaningful outcomes for the peoples of the region. It would make spending more efficient and allow multiple donors to leverage the benefits of individual projects. It would not seek to align any individual donor's aid objectives with those of other donors, though such partnerships would be welcome were they to occur organically.

ODA must always meet recipients' needs. The magnificent buildings that exceed the management and maintenance capacities of the aid recipients, the roads to nowhere, the professional development programs for officials that ignore rather than prevent endemic corruption, the education of health workers who lack clinics and equipment, the training of teachers who have no classrooms to accommodate their students – these failures do nothing to improve the wellbeing of Pacific communities. They can be prevented through coordination and planning.

WHY IT WILL WORK: Pacific communities, like those in South-East Asia, prefer collaborative problem solving. When ODA programs are imposed by donors from overseas, with minimal ownership or agency on a local level, the result is inertia. Donors – or their consultants – arrive, deliver what was promised, and depart, with little thought to ongoing implementation. Instead of being energised, the beneficiaries are often left disengaged.

Donors and recipients alike need to share accountability. Donors need discipline in their program planning and follow-up. Recipients must take responsibility for the long-term success of these programs. Few Pacific aid meetings focus on coordinating inputs, sharing success stories and embedding accountability.

Some will argue rightly that, despite the creation of many Pacific institutions since World War II, there is little sense of common purpose in the region, and where it does exist it is problem-focused rather than solutions-driven. But Pacific nations must be more cohesive, cooperative and proactive to survive and prosper. A focus on results, rather than on aspirational development concepts, will help to build that sense of common purpose.

Signals about intention and good faith are important in diplomacy globally, but particularly in the highly communal and locally focused cultures of the Pacific. Australia's diplomats in the Pacific are eager, hardworking and respected by their hosts. They are good at the bilateral work. Yet despite their efforts, Australia often appears condescending and overbearing in the region, generating resigned acceptance from Pacific leaders rather than enthusiastic collaboration. The countries of the Pacific want engagement, and would love Australia to "step up" genuinely to the task. But the leadership they seek involves cooperation, dialogue, understanding and, above all, respect. Most Pacific nations are not interested in being a site for Australia or the United States to conduct their strategic battles with China. They are interested in improving outcomes for their citizens, who are among the most aid-dependent in the world.

The Pacific is a region of many players whose competitive jostling increasingly hinders economic and social progress. A multilateral initiative that brings key actors together to focus on the wellbeing of the region's residents will meet a real need.

Should China be included in this conference? Certainly. Australia is more likely to limit strategic competition and confrontation in the Pacific through discussion and engagement with China than through ill-conceived efforts at containment. China's participation in consultation over the Pacific and its future is far preferable to its traditional reliance on bilateral diplomacy.

In South-East Asia, consultative fora such as the ASEAN Regional Forum and the East Asia Summit work, mainly because they involve everyone, and there is a cultural preference for dialogue. The Pacific shares this emphasis on dialogue. An annual conference for donors and recipients, focusing on objectives, programs and outcomes, would substantially improve the lives of the peoples of the Pacific and clean up the mess around ODA in which the region is mired.

THE RESPONSE: The Department of Foreign Affairs and Trade would not say whether it supported the convening of an annual Pacific donors' conference, but noted that mechanisms already exist for promoting dialogue and coordination. "Australia participates in regional information sharing and coordination in the Pacific, including coordination of development assistance," a spokesperson said. "The pre-eminent regional event is the annual Pacific Islands Forum Leaders Meeting, which brings together Pacific leaders including our prime minister. China is a dialogue partner and the United Nations is an observer at this event."

Reviews

City on Fire: The Fight for Hong Kong
Antony Dapiran
Scribe Publications

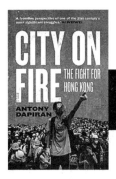

On 1 July 2020, China enforced a national security law in Hong Kong, which swept locals, who had lived for decades within the relative shelter of the common law system, further than ever under Beijing's rule. The city's vivacious atmosphere quietened almost overnight as it became clear that the vaguely defined law could leave those who break it in prison for life. Residents deleted their social media pages and text messages. Shop and café owners peeled down the pro-protest yellow propaganda that had spread across the metropolis like butter. The first arrests were made. As the city's leader, Carrie Lam, watched the rise of the Chinese flag, it was clear the old Hong Kong had melted and a new era had begun.

In the aftermath, Antony Dapiran wondered if his book *City on Fire*, which was only published in March, was still relevant. "Things have moved so quickly and beyond anyone's expectations," the Hong Kong–based corporate lawyer and author tells me.

City on Fire, however, is about the opposite of this white-out, according to Dapiran. It memorialises the fateful events in the territory in 2019, which saw millions flock to the streets to protest what they argued were increasing incursions on Hong Kong's autonomy, presenting President Xi Jinping with one of the most open displays of political dissent on Chinese soil since Tiananmen.

The book – Dapiran's second, after 2017's *City of Protest*, also about Hong Kong – is a detailed portrait of each of the key protests and events that sparked the 2019 crisis, and a reflection on how they relate to the city's post-handover history. "To remember [how the community felt at the time] is important as we move into this new era," Dapiran said in an interview, "and in the search for a new language under the national security law."

Critics say the city's leaders have already used the new law to attempt to suppress opposition in upcoming elections. Some in academia and the media say the law has increased pressure to avoid displays of sympathy for the movement – many fear losing their jobs if they speak out.

Police have also tried to stop protesters from gathering to commemorate protest anniversaries. On 2 July, the Hong Kong government declared the popular slogan "Liberate Hong Kong, revolution of our times" in breach of the new law. "So much of what the protest movement does is to self-mythologise, to build collective memories ... the national security law is trying to ban that, starting with the slogans. The CCP is good at controlling memory and narrative," Dapiran says.

Hong Kong writer Karen Cheung says there has long been a "crazy impulse" among local writers and artists to see their work as archiving the period from the handover until 2047, when the "one country, two systems" policy expires. Dapiran, who attended so many protests one was bound to bump into him if out reporting, aligns with that tradition. He seeks to capture the culture of the protests and the evolving demands of the protesters as the months-long demonstrations wear on; the book is propelled by this energy. It delves into the art that, for a time, fluttered through nearly every city overpass, the ubiquitous colourful Post-it Note "Lennon Walls", the crowdsourced origins of the protest song "Glory to Hong Kong". It explains the slow descent into the "if we burn, you burn with us" attitude and the nihilistic desperation of the frontline "braves" who used homemade shields, Molotov cocktails and even catapults in stand-offs with riot police.

With Hong Kong's universities labs of dissent innovation, the movement relied on a decentralised leadership structure coordinated through social media. The protesters' "be water" strategy involved luring police into formation; then they would quickly disappear through the city's concrete architecture after voting on smartphone Reddit-like apps about where to reappear.

Dapiran argues that these tactics have given them global influence. From Black Lives Matter to Extinction Rebellion, protesters have been making reference to Hong Kong's yellow-helmeted youth. Dapiran is in awe of their passion, and makes no pretence of being a removed outsider: "I find it very inspiring that a people who had a reputation for being politically apathetic … get onto the streets, put their bodies physically on the line and keep fighting for what they believe in." It was this theatre, he suggests, that put the protests so firmly on the world stage, and fashioned the city into a "domino" symbolising China's growing international influence in the minds of Western politicians: "Hong Kong is a city that's enjoyed rights and freedoms on the very border of a place, like West Berlin did during the Cold War – that's a potent image."

But he argues in *City on Fire* that it has also made Hong Kong a pawn, as others find ways to use its story for their own purposes. "That's part of the tragedy."

Since Dapiran takes his perspective from the demonstrators, the book does not offer a view from inside the central government in Beijing, the local administration in Hong Kong or the police force. The consequences of the streak of anti-mainlander hatred, which arguably stained the protests, is noted but not explored in detail. While Dapiran does explain its complex origins, it was extraordinary to see mainland Chinese people in the vicinity of protests or just out on the streets face possible violence and harassment for speaking Mandarin rather than the local Cantonese language. Some have said this undermined the possibility of solidarity with those on the mainland and made it easier for Chinese state media to vilify the protesters.

Yet *City on Fire* does not aim to be a staid, uninvolved history. It situates the reader on those steaming streets to remind them that in 2019, in the height of summer, millions of Hong Kongers gambled everything to try to take back their city and their freedom. Would Australians do the same?

Primrose Riordan

Capitalism, Alone: The
Future of the System
That Rules the World
Branko Milanovic
Belknap Press

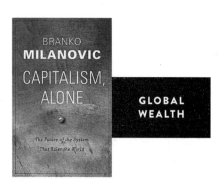

I n *Capitalism, Alone*, Branko Milanovic outlines the weaknesses of capitalism as an economic system. His analysis encompasses two competing forms – liberal capitalism as epitomised by the United States and political capitalism as epitomised by China – both of which he sees as flawed. They result in income inequality, reduced intergenerational mobility and the concentration of political power with the elite, particularly in the liberal version. These weaknesses arise from a system that fosters social divisions due to the private provision of services such as education and health, which leads to resistance to higher taxes. Milanovic

also offers suggestions on how capitalism, especially its liberal form, might be improved.

Capitalism, Alone was published in September 2019, in the era before COVID-19. The pandemic, which has hit the global economy in unprecedented ways, highlights the weaknesses in capitalism that Milanovic outlines, placing his book in a more urgent light.

There is no doubt that the global contraction in economic growth caused by COVID-19 will be unprecedented. It will dwarf the global financial crisis and the Great Recession that followed partly because, despite their names, these crises were not global. This public health crisis is. Countries have mandated varying forms of lockdown, populations have complied to varying degrees and the transmission of COVID-19 differs across nations. But despite divergences in policies, compliance and outcomes, all countries are experiencing slowed growth. According to the World Bank, in 2020 global gross domestic product is forecast to contract by between 5 and 8 per cent, most countries will enter into recession, and per capita income will decrease in the highest proportion of countries globally since 1870.

Domestic lockdown policies are not the main contributor to the downturn. The cause is the spread of a virus that compels people to change their social interactions to avoid illness and hence their demand for goods and services, independent of government directives. The labour force contracts; in addition, sick people cannot work. These effects combine to cause substantial interruption to the global economy through supply and demand channels, the disruption of transportation networks and the sudden halt in the flow of people across borders for tourism, business and education. It turns out that a healthy population predicates a healthy economy.

The pandemic reinforces Milanovic's analysis of capitalism's flaws. The waves of the virus affect those least able to afford it – youth, minority groups and women who work in service industries, who have either lost their jobs or are on the front line caring for others, putting themselves and their families at risk – thereby exacerbating inequality in income and wealth across generations. It also accentuates inequality in education and health. The challenges posed by remote learning, a lack of access to technology (particularly among the poor) and an increased reliance on parents to teach – as well as the lack of opportunity to develop professional and social networks in university classrooms and campuses – will inevitably lead to at least short-term educational disadvantage for the young, compared with previous generations. In many countries, unequal access to healthcare and an inadequate income safety net means that sick people need to go to work. In developing countries, these problems are even more severe, with World Bank estimates that between 40 and 60 million more people will enter extreme poverty in 2020.

The macroeconomic policy responses to support the population through the pandemic inevitably and rightly require massive increases in government debt and the central banks' intervention in asset markets, as interest rates in many countries sit close to zero. Unfortunately, asset holders – that is, the wealthy – are the beneficiaries of interventions in asset markets, while the repayment of the debt will fall mostly to the young. Both of these factors exacerbate intergenerational inequality.

Perversely, the stimulus required to avert economic disaster means that we can afford the scale of investment needed to address the issues Milanovic highlights. The pandemic has shown that healthcare needs to be a universal public good, not the choice or burden of an individual. A critical lesson is the need for adequate healthcare in both developed and developing countries, and in particular the ability for the rapid detection, treatment and suppression of new diseases wherever they emerge. Viruses do not respect borders or income level. The cost to the global economy would have been much lower if global healthcare had been a priority before 2019.

The scale of stimulus necessary also provides an opportunity to equalise some of the imbalances developing between generations. Although Milanovic does not address this in his book, the critical issue for the young is climate change, and those working on reducing emissions have myriad projects and plans ready to be executed.

Examples include developing the infrastructure for renewable energy, and developing smart and flexible transport infrastructure such as electric car networks – which could prove particularly valuable given that public transport will be a less favoured option for travel until the pandemic is contained.

The recession of 2020 is different from those in the past. Many of the losses are being accrued by women who work in roles with high levels of social contact. Economic stimulus can also protect the advances made in gender equality while benefitting low-income groups. The obvious area for investment is education, a key contributor to productivity growth. Governments should fund the rethinking of traditional models of education that has been kickstarted by the pandemic, including through investment in universal fast internet, and providing low-income households with access to technology, such as computers.

The international economy is undergoing massive structural change. However, smart stimulus expenditure in climate infrastructure, health and education, and the lessons learnt from flexible working arrangements and the use of technologies such as Zoom, might just lead to a surge in global productivity that has been sadly lacking since the mid-2000s. Many measures are consistent with the reforms Milanovic proposes in *Capitalism, Alone*. Due to the tragic impacts of COVID-19, these reforms are more probable now than when Milanovic published his book.

Renée Fry-McKibbin

The Road: Uprising in West Papua
John Martinkus
Black Inc.

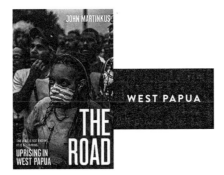

From January to July 2020, more than sixty-five West Papuans were detained, put on trial and jailed for up to seventeen years. Their crimes? Protesting against racism and raising a flag. West Papuans' attempts to salvage their dignity as humans and their self-determination as a people has led to indictments of "treason", "criminal conspiracy" and "incitement".

This criminalisation of Papuan human rights activists is only the latest instance in West Papuans' history of oppression under Indonesian rule – a history that includes their loss of lands and freedoms, their subjugation to physical and psychological abuse, and their unfulfilled demands for self-determination. This volatile history forms the core of John Martinkus's *The Road*. With experience reporting from Iraq, Afghanistan, Sri Lanka, Burma, Timor-Leste and Aceh, Martinkus, a four-time Walkley-nominated investigative reporter, is no stranger to extreme violence and gross injustice. Yet he reveals he has never seen "a people more systematically oppressed and isolated than the West Papuans".

In West Papua, random killings, sudden arrests and egregious torture are not just authorised by the Indonesian state but routinely celebrated in horrific spectacles of violence – the use of snakes as instruments of interrogation, the burning of bodies with white phosphorous grenades, the sexual abuse of indigenous Papuan women by military forces. These events often lie beyond the purview (and priorities) of the international media, partly because access to West Papua is notoriously restricted for journalists and researchers, both domestic and foreign.

And yet the West Papua conflict is far from just an Indonesian issue. The global community – Australia, the United States, the United Nations and multinational conglomerates, among others – is deeply complicit. This manifests in geopolitical alignments that prioritise national interests over minority rights, exploitative corporate collusion and, most importantly, a glaring silence in the face of the longest-running political conflict of the South Pacific. The story Martinkus tells is one of localised violence and oppression, but it is also a narrative of international betrayal and abandonment.

Named for the Trans-Papua Highway, a controversial project promoted by the Indonesian government to support regional economic development, *The Road* takes us through a series of events that have shaped West Papuans' history of suffering under Indonesian rule. These include the region's illicit occupation in the 1960s, the state-military-corporate troika systematically plundering Papua's resources, and the violent attacks and displacement suffered by those who oppose development projects imposed on them by the government. The book shows how fear, intimidation and vulnerability haunt the lives of West Papua's "second-class and expendable citizens", who are routinely exposed to the arbitrary violence of the state and its omnipresent military and police apparatus.

This "slow-motion genocide", however, is not all that we encounter along the road. Just as important is the resilience, courage and determination of West Papuans who continue to fight for their country, resources and rights, increasingly in alliance with politically aware young Indonesians. This resilience manifests in the intensifying pro-independence guerrilla movement in the Highlands, the ongoing call from the exiled diaspora for a referendum through the United Nations, the exposure of human rights abuses by lawyers and activists, and the rise of an educated and articulate Papuan generation who share an overwhelming desire to "right a historic wrong".

Seminal quotes from key figures help us navigate the troubled terrain of West Papua's political landscape. We hear, for instance, from exiled independence activist Benny Wenda, theologian and anthropologist Benny Giay, Indonesia's Coordinating Minister for Political, Security and Law Wiranto, and exiled human-rights lawyer Veronica Koman. The book recounts eventful moments of West Papua's past and present in all their harrowing poignancy. But its focus on major events in West Papua's history and political struggle obscures the everyday experiences, desires and conundrums of its people. Between these dramatic moments lies the chronic violence too mundane to make the headlines and the endurance of life lived in the teeth of settler-colonial dispossession.

It is this far less spectacular daily experience that I encountered during my fieldwork between 2013 and 2019 in the West Papuan district of Merauke, where Martinkus begins his book. Here, as elsewhere in the province, vast swathes of land customarily owned by indigenous Papuans are being privatised and cleared at an unprecedented rate to make way for palm oil and logging operations. It is not independence or autonomy that constitute local inhabitants' primary aspirations, but far more immediate needs: feeding their children, finding clean water, and maintaining social ties amid growing community fragmentation and cultural erosion. Life in this remote place is shaped as much by resistance to predatory state and corporate interests as by a profound ambivalence over what capitalism, modernity and development can offer. Roads and plantations incarnate these predatory interests – but they nonetheless conjure for many Papuan men, women and children the promise of wealth, education and social mobility.

At the same time, the realm of daily life is also where Papuans exercise the kind of resilience that Martinkus examines in the context of political self-determination. In Merauke, Papuans walk the forest with their kin, teaching their children the songs and stories of the landscape, celebrating the plants and animals that animate it and commemorating the ancestral spirits that dwell within it. These mundane activities constitute fundamental acts of survival for West Papuans as they strive to sustain their cultures, values and identities. They merit the same kind of attention as the struggle for political self-determination that *The Road* privileges.

Martinkus's epilogue offers a glimpse of the contradictions that characterise everyday life in West Papua today. The transmigrants he describes arriving in Jayapura, the capital of the Indonesian province of Papua, are part of Indonesia's attempt to turn the region's indigenous people into a minority. In Merauke district, for instance, Papuans now represent less than 60 per cent of the population. And yet as Martinkus observes, transmigrants are themselves often poor and afraid, and arrive with modest expectations – farming the

land or opening a small kiosk. Their futures in West Papua remain deeply precarious. Likewise, the roads – material and imaginative – that West Papuans travel today are defined as much by their protracted struggle for political independence as by the uncertain promises and possibilities of daily life.

Attendance to the everyday does not undermine the importance of tracing and highlighting the ongoing pursuit of political freedom, as Martinkus does. Rather, it foregrounds that, for many West Papuans, it is never easy to choose which road to follow. These choices manifest as much in Papuans' political stances as in what they eat, what language they opt to speak and what they wear. Through these small acts, Papuans retrace ancestral roads of belonging and being, forged through custom and tradition. At the same time, these roads are sites of tentative experimentation, where Papuans creatively fashion new ways of becoming Papuan, both within and against Indonesian rule.

Sophie Chao

*The Storm Before
the Calm: America's
Discord, the Coming
Crisis of the 2020s, and
the Triumph Beyond*
George Friedman
Black Inc.

Optimistic accounts of contemporary America are in
short supply, but George
Friedman has written sev-
eral. In each of his readable
books (most are *New York Times*
bestsellers), he has constructed a
compelling case for believing that the
United States has some distance to
run. That argument is given a histor-
ical anchor in his latest release, *The
Storm Before the Calm*. While the main
text was written between 2015 and
2019, the addition of a foreword to
the Australian edition, written in July
2020, allows him to address COVID-19
and the proof it affords his thesis.

That thesis is captured in
the title: America endures stormy
weather (riots, depression, war)
which inevitably gives way to calm
(prosperity, freedom, innovation).
It has ever been thus, he argues,
and ever will be: if we understand
the cycles of US history, we can
better grasp the nation's future.
"The current storm," he writes, "is
nothing more than what is normal
for this time in America's history
and our lives."

The first part of the book
outlines why America has been such
a success. The second describes how
and why its triumphs will continue.

Why successful? The United
States has three things going
for it: its government is entirely
invented; its people are mostly
immigrants dedicated to continual
reinvention; and they are afforded
the geopolitical space in which to
do this. Regime, citizens and land.
"All of these created a platform,"
writes Friedman, "not only for rapid
growth but for managing the growth."
This exceptional and evolving
combination continues to give
Americans distinct advantages
over their geostrategic opponents.

Russians have land, but have
been continually hampered by

a series of regimes incapable of reinvention – one system arises, oppresses and dies, only for another to follow suit. Russian society produces very little entrepreneurialism: oligarchs, yes; Henry Ford, no. The land on which Russian political experiments must take place is prey to invasion from the West; the United States enjoys an enviable security by comparison.

China is surrounded by nations that do not quite trust it. Its political and economic innovation is more borrowed than organic. Its governments of the last 100 years have tilted from chaotic to authoritarian. Chinese communism, an adapted Western import, seeks to mediate all technological development, whereas Washington had very little to do with the success of Silicon Valley. China's huge, low-wage workforce means it can create iPhone jobs, but not Steve Jobs.

Neither Russia nor China attracts immigrants. Even people who hate America, Friedman reminds us, want to send their children there.

A Hungarian émigré to the United States, married to an Australian, Friedman is keen to extol the enduring attraction of an immigrant nation. The Europe he left behind – though he remains a popular public intellectual in Hungary – asks him who he is. America, in contrast, wants to know what he does. That liberation from blood and soil, and elevation to a realm where work and ideas define identity and success, remains central to the author's self-perception. And he wants to evangelise his experience.

Why and how will this success continue? In the book's second half, Friedman identifies "two very orderly cycles" of American history – the institutional and the socioeconomic. Understand these, he tells us, and one's faith in the US experiment will be restored: "This is how the United States was designed to evolve."

The institutional cycle "runs its course roughly every eighty years", Friedman writes. Each emerges from war. Thus, 1787 to 1865, 1865 to 1945, and 1945 to the 2020s are comparable periods in which US institutions were invented to keep pace with the restless energy of the people, fractured under the weight of new restlessness and were reinvented.

The third institutional cycle, concluding now, is central to his argument. During and after World

War II, deference to experts and technocrats transformed the productive capacities and wealth of the United States. Technological innovation, in everything from whitegoods to military hardware, kept pace with the demands of a victorious people. But by the 1960s and 1970s, government technocrats were starting to fail as social engineers. American society began to fracture and its economy to weaken: "What started as splendid ideas eventually wore out as the society changed."

By the 2010s, the Great Recession and defenestration of America's manufacturing base had brought economic experts and technocratic elites into disrepute. Friedman is especially hard on the universities ("the center of gravity of the technocracy") for perpetuating this managerial class. In 2016, Donald Trump performed his role in the cycle by calling this smug elite to account. By 2025 to 2030, Friedman predicts, institutional reinvention will begin a confident new cycle, which in turn will collapse around 2100–10. The COVID-19 pandemic has put the cycle "on steroids", hastening the institutional reinvention

(not least of American federalism) that punctuates US history.

What makes our decade unique is the ending of not just an institutional cycle but also a socioeconomic one. This second cycle, according to Friedman, runs every fifty years. The two cycles have never ended simultaneously. The creative destruction it will involve, he assures us, will be a wonder to behold, "transforming" how society works. The election of 2028 ("2032 at the outside"), predicts Friedman confidently, will mark the beginning of the end of technocracy and its replacement by a more egalitarian, commonsensical and inclusive governing philosophy. This struggle will be "grim" but will ultimately end well.

The last cyclical transition occurred when Ronald Reagan changed economic policy in 1981. This worked until the system fell into disrepair and recession in the 2010s. Institutional *and* socio-economic reinvention will happen simultaneously and symbiotically as its replacement emerges in the 2020s and 2030s. Failure will be followed by creativity. Storm will give way to calm. Why? Because it always has. Look at the pattern, insists Friedman.

"The cycle is working itself out in the murky depths."

A respected expert in geopolitical forecasting, Friedman is read more as prophet than historian. He wears both hats well in this book. Too many academics remain rooted to one era or cause; too few range from the past into even vague contours of the future. Friedman corrects some of these deficiencies with his approach.

The imposition of patterns on American history is not novel. Some important scholars have surveyed the last 240-plus years and heard distinctive rhythms. In 1986, Arthur M. Schlesinger Jr identified "cycles of American history", but resisted the confident forecasting Friedman specialises in. In 1982, Samuel P. Huntington located a "gap" between ideas and the institutions needed to advance them that has echoes in Friedman's cycles. And, of course, Karl Marx said history moved in a clear and predictable direction. Despite assimilating much of their logic and approach, Friedman discusses none of them here.

Politics in the United States has a mathematical regularity – elections occur every second November, and representatives, presidents and governors, and senators are elected every two, four and six years respectively. So there is a certain attraction to seeing events unfold in patterns, as Friedman does. US presidencies have a neat, predictable stop-start timeframe that Australian prime ministerships do not. Friedman's five socioeconomic cycles are all named for the presidents who initiated them: Washington, Jackson, Hayes, Franklin D. Roosevelt and Reagan.

While I share much of the author's optimism about America's prospects, I am sceptical that renewal follows the neat timetable he constructs. The US Constitution was intended as "a machine that would go of itself". However, it has been the nation's sheer good luck in getting the right leaders at the right moments – a function of fortune rather than of orderly cycles – that accounts for much of its success. Men and women do not make the weather; they do make politics.

Friedman has given us a positive account of US political, economic and social development, and is optimistic about the nation's prospects. In a time of Trump and plague, this happy outlook is a rare commodity. As such, his arguments demand the widest possible airing. Without interventions like his, we are in danger of a scholarly discourse of unrelenting gloom. In *The Storm Before the Calm*, Friedman has offered us a timely reminder that US successes far outweigh US failures – and that the odds on this continuing look strong.

Timothy J. Lynch

Correspondence

"Drawing the Line"
by Kim McGrath

John Hewson

Kim McGrath's "Drawing the Line" (AFA9: *Spy vs Spy*) is a fair and balanced account of one of the most sordid episodes in the history of Australian foreign relations. It took place early this century due to the desperation of the Howard government; it occurred mostly to benefit a few of its corporate mates; it was immoral and illegal in its concept and execution; and it was not effectively exposed and addressed by subsequent Labor governments, with the Coalition sustaining the cover-up to this day.

The accusations run that Australia, one of the world's richest countries, spied on one of the world's poorest countries, Timor-Leste, to gain advantage in the Timor Sea boundary negotiations, where the spoils were extremely lucrative oil and gas reserves. Specifically, the Howard government authorised the Australian Secret Intelligence Service (ASIS) to bug Timor-Leste's federal ministerial offices, diverting crucial intelligence resources from the so-called "war on terror" (in which obvious failures occurred over the Bali bombings and at our Indonesian embassy), then carried it out under the shameful cover of an aid program and sought to use the information obtained to exploit Timor-Leste in the negotiations.

The issue of spying arose because the economic zones of Australia and Timor-Leste overlap. Rather than adopt the accepted international practice of drawing a boundary at the midpoint, Australia offered a number of alternatives to ensure preferential access to the natural resources. But, after some clever political and international legal manoeuvring by the Timorese, the irony was that the final treaty was set essentially at that midpoint.

McGrath has presented an excellent, comprehensive and readable summary of the various events, from the espionage activity in 2004 through to the prosecution of the retired ASIS agent known as "Witness K" and his lawyer, Bernard Collaery, initiated by Attorney-General Christian Porter under Turnbull in June 2018 – almost immediately after the formal signing of the treaty. The charges were "conspiring to reveal classified information" – essentially communicating with ABC journalists – and the matter is still proceeding through the ACT Supreme Court.

As McGrath writes, the prosecution "throws a spotlight on the nexus between politics and intelligence, and the unfettered power of ministers in Australia's intelligence regime" and "shows that opportunities for an operative to challenge a direction to perform an immoral or illegal act are limited and likely to be career-ending". Clinton Fernandes of the University of New South Wales puts it accurately: "Basically, what the government is trying to do is prosecute people for revealing its own crimes."

Ian Cunliffe, a lawyer and former senior federal public servant with an enviable record in law reform and intelligence and security, wrote in the *Australian Financial Review* in August 2020: "We all know that ASIS did the bugging. If it wants Collaery's head on a platter, the Commonwealth should be required to acknowledge its own crime in open court, and to defend its actions."

The case of Witness K is a very sorry tale, in which an intelligence operative has deep moral and legal reservations about the tasks he is being expected to perform or support by his political and bureaucratic masters, and finds himself "constructively dismissed". Moreover, when he seeks to raise his experience internally, he is referred to a lawyer "vetted" by ASIS, but under the *Intelligence Services Act 2001* is unable to brief him fully on the detail. How fair is it that, some sixteen years after the bugging, with the treaty finalised, and following raids on his home and that of his lawyer, he and his lawyer are charged, and dragged through a court process, mostly in secret, while his political and bureaucratic masters who sat at the highest levels of our government walk free?

Worse still, some of those masters have since been rewarded, taking up positions with their corporate mates who benefited from their illegality and immorality, leaving their successors in government to fund and run that court case simply to cover up what they did.

These events highlight the need for more-effective scrutiny, from outside the executive, of our intelligence services and their operations, as well as greater accountability from senior individuals in their ranks. They also show the need to clean up our politics, to remove the undue influence of special interests through reform of campaign funding and other financial support for and lobbying of our politicians. We need clear limits on, and transparency about, elected representatives' involvement with and engagement by such interests during and after their political career.

As a minimum, the Joint Committee on Intelligence and Security should operate more along US Congressional lines – this committee should have complete access to the regular intelligence briefings provided to government, with full knowledge of the intelligence assets used (such as corporates and other institutions and agencies). It needs the powers of a royal commission to investigate, pursue evidence and report possible illegality in relation to both current and past intelligence activities, and with important formal and informal obligations to report to the Australian Parliament.

With trust in governments having collapsed over recent decades, it is now an electoral imperative to ensure proper scrutiny and accountability. Our system of government should do, and be perceived to do, what is right and fair and in our national interest, rather than favouring narrow special interests.

So much legislation has been passed in the name of national security in recent years, and intelligence institutions and agencies, along with ministerial responsibilities, have been shuffled and reshuffled. The composition and purpose of our intelligence community – including the rights and obligations of its various parts – are almost indecipherable.

I strongly support historian Peter Edwards' position that the next Independent Intelligence Review (due around 2022) be upgraded to a royal commission in order to enable a "reassessment of the structures, legislation and operations of the whole intelligence community". This commission should work to a broader definition of our national security, which includes health, environmental and other non-traditional threats to our long-term interests.

John Hewson is a professor at the Australian National University and a former leader of the Liberal Party and the federal opposition.

Jenny McAllister

n the 1980 election campaign, Ronald Reagan famously asked Americans if they were better off than four years earlier. It was a question voters could answer with their payslips, and experts could weigh in with economic data and informed analysis.

In the lead-up to the 2004 election, John Kerry asked if Americans thought they were safer than three years earlier. It was an important question in the wake of 9/11, but how were voters to answer? How could they attribute this outcome to government policy? Was national security expenditure being used well? Were the impositions on personal liberty and privacy necessary?

Security is a core task of government, but questions about it are difficult for citizens to answer. Much of national security decision-making is, necessarily, secret. However, that secrecy is in permanent tension with legitimate democratic expectations of accountability.

As the American academic Dennis F. Thompson put it:

> The dilemma of accountability may be thought of as a political version of the Heisenberg Uncertainty Principle. Just as physicists cannot measure a particle's position and momentum at the same time ... so citizens cannot evaluate some policies and processes because the act of evaluating defeats the policy or undermines the process.

Intelligence oversight bodies help mediate this tension between secrecy and accountability. They work to maintain a culture of trust that is necessary for intelligence agencies to operate effectively in a democracy. Strong oversight bodies should not be seen as opposing national security agencies – instead they are an essential part of the institutions charged with keeping us safe.

Kim McGrath concludes her piece by noting some of the gaps in Australia's intelligence oversight arrangements. Reform of these arrangements is well overdue.

The key institutions were created more than three decades ago by the Hawke government, following the Hope Royal Commission. The Parliamentary Joint Committee on Intelligence and Security (PJCIS) reviews national security legislation, examines agencies' administration and expenditure, and performs other policy review functions (such as its recent inquiry into press freedoms).

The Inspector General of Intelligence and Security (IGIS) is an independent statutory office holder who has powers analogous to a standing royal commission to investigate the legality and propriety of particular operations and activities.

The last major update to these arrangements was the creation of the Independent National Security Legislation Monitor (INSLM) by the Rudd and Gillard governments in 2010.

A lot has changed since then. We've seen the creation of a new Home Affairs portfolio and the addition of new agencies to the national intelligence community structure. The volume of national security legislation has swelled. More agencies than ever before have access to intelligence capabilities and functions, and those capabilities have been augmented by new technologies for collecting and analysing data.

Oversight must keep pace with capabilities if intelligence agencies are to enjoy the public trust they need to operate effectively. As McGrath notes, there is no shortage of proposals for reform, just a lack of political will to implement them.

In 2016, Prime Minister Malcolm Turnbull tasked Stephen Merchant and Michael L'Estrange with reviewing our intelligence services. The Independent Intelligence Review reported the next year and identified oversight as a priority area for reform. The government seemingly accepted all of the review's recommendations, yet little progress was made in implementing those involving oversight. Instead, work was apparently shelved pending the outcome of another review being conducted by Dennis Richardson. That inquiry reported last year, but its findings have not been released publicly or responded to by the government.

The lack of action is a mistake.

To address this, I introduced a private senator's bill in February 2019. It builds on previous similar bills by Senators John Faulkner and Penny Wong, and incorporates many of the recommendations of the Independent Intelligence Review. The review made sensible and modest proposals that plug clear gaps in our oversight arrangements. Changes in administrative arrangements, for instance, mean that the IGIS and PJCIS do not currently have oversight of all the agencies in the Australian intelligence community (including the Department of Home Affairs). This should be fixed. There are legislative barriers to the INSLM, IGIS and PJCIS working collaboratively that should be removed. The proposed reforms would also allow the PJCIS to initiate inquiries without waiting for a referral from the prime minister, and to refer matters to the IGIS that the committee was not able to investigate itself.

These are clear, simple improvements. There is no apparent impediment to the government implementing them – either through the private senator's bill, or through new legislation if it preferred.

Other avenues for reform of our oversight arrangements also merit consideration, but this is a good place to start. In considering future reforms, though, we should remember that there is no perfect configuration of oversight arrangements. Different jurisdictions have tried different models with differing effects. None is infallible.

What is perhaps most important is fostering the culture of trust that oversight bodies are meant to protect. This is a task that involves us all.

Jenny McAllister is a Labor senator for New South Wales and a member of the Parliamentary Joint Committee on Intelligence and Security.

Andrew Zammit

n October 2004, the same month that Australian Secret Intelligence Service (ASIS) operatives allegedly installed listening devices in Timor-Leste's cabinet room, Dr Coral Bell gave a prescient warning. One of Australia's most renowned scholars of international relations, Bell argued that "giving Australia the lion's share of the oil revenues that East Timor must depend on for its very survival ... may be in the interests of local oil companies, but it is contrary to the national interest".

Kim McGrath's important essay shows how this played out. Australia's excessive maritime claims in the Timor Gap negotiations were both morally flawed and a self-inflicted policy failure. They harmed Australia's relations with the world's newest nation-state and embroiled our intelligence agencies in controversy. They also ended up undermining Australia's critiques of China's undue claims in the South China Sea.

McGrath's essay endorses historian Peter Edwards' call for the next Independent Intelligence Review to be upgraded to a royal commission, adding that the Witness K scandal should be included in its terms of reference. This conclusion is compelling, for three reasons.

First, a royal commission could resolve the factual disputes that surround the scandal. The Inspector-General of Intelligence and Security has emphatically denied that Witness K ever raised an operation in Timor with its office, stating that there is "no record of any former or current ASIS officer having raised concerns with us about alleged Australian government activity in East Timor". Similarly, former ASIO, Department of Foreign Affairs and Trade and Department of Defence head Dennis Richardson has disputed that any such operation would have diverted ASIS resources from counterterrorism. These two assertions are at odds with key claims being made on behalf of Witness K and Bernard Collaery, but the trial's secrecy means that the truth remains unclear. Moreover, the trial presumably focuses on the narrow question of Collaery's alleged wrongdoing, whereas a royal commission could help to uncover what happened throughout the scandal and, without undermining security concerns, establish a public record.

Second, factual disputes aside, there are good reasons to believe a great injustice has occurred. As McGrath's essay shows, there is a long history of unjust Australian policy towards Timor-Leste, going back to the Whitlam and Fraser governments' acquiescence to Indonesia's 1975 invasion, which makes the Witness K allegations credible and worthy of independent investigation.

Third, the Witness K scandal poses a more significant threat to the public standing of Australia's intelligence services than do other recent controversies. This is clear from the number of high-profile individuals speaking out, including former New South Wales Supreme Court judge Anthony Whealy and former Independent National Security Legislation Monitor (INSLM) Bret Walker. Both are authoritative voices on national security and justice; Whealy oversaw terrorism trials that involved the *National Security Information (Criminal and Civil Proceedings) Act 2004*, the same legislation which has made the Witness K and Collaery prosecutions so secretive.

The prosecutions perpetuate the scandal for ASIS, at a time when the intelligence agencies have an increasingly important role to play as global order deteriorates. This adds urgency to Edwards' appeal for a royal commission and McGrath's call for it to examine the Witness K affair. A commission could help uncover the truth, rectify what appears to be a great injustice and address the scandal's impact on the public legitimacy of Australia's intelligence agencies as they face the rapidly evolving threats outlined in the essays by Anne-Marie Brady, Danielle Cave and Andrew Davies in the same issue.

McGrath's essay also calls for boosting the role of the Parliamentary Joint Committee on Intelligence and Security. This would be valuable. Former Labor MP John Faulkner presented a detailed argument for it in his 2014 paper *Surveillance, Intelligence and Accountability: An Australian Story*. Another option could be for the new INSLM, Grant Donaldson, to resume the former INSLM James Renwick's review into the *National Security Information Act*, which was delayed by COVID-19 and then halted when Renwick's term ended in June 2020.

Yet proposals for improving accountability also have inherent limits. The history of Australia's intelligence agencies is scattered with the regular creation of new accountability mechanisms but also ongoing dissatisfaction with those same mechanisms, because they risk amounting to legalistic solutions for political problems. This is due to a deeper issue, which McGrath's essay raises: "Who determines what is proper?"

In a democracy, intelligence agencies have necessary roles to play and ultimately answer to elected leaders. Governments decide their policy goals, and the agencies provide information to help achieve those goals. It is hard to imagine an arrangement that would keep intelligence agencies under democratic control but avoid the risk that elected leaders might make disastrous decisions. As McGrath's essay reminds us, Australian governments have, tragically, proven willing to make injurious decisions towards Timor-Leste time and again.

Andrew Zammit is a PhD candidate at Monash University and a researcher at Victoria University, focusing on terrorism and security issues.

Kim McGrath responds

Since the publication of my essay on the prosecution of former spy Witness K and his lawyer, Bernard Collaery, for revealing allegations that Australia spied on the Timorese during maritime boundary negotiations in 2004, the Australian Labor Party has condemned the bugging operation and the prosecutions.

In an interview with *Crikey* in August, Labor leader Anthony Albanese said, "What happened in East Timor was wrong. It should never have happened." He was "very concerned about transparency in this case – the idea that there should be a prosecution of a whistle-blower, for what's a shameful part of Australia's history, is simply wrong". When it was put to Albanese that his comments were the most forthright on the bugging issue from Labor, he said, "Well, you should have asked me before."

Albanese's condemnation of the spying and prosecutions is welcome. But why should the Labor leader need to be "asked" to comment on what former Liberal leader John Hewson describes in his response to my essay as "one of the most sordid episodes in the history of Australian foreign relations"?

The ALP's coyness to date about condemning the misuse of our intelligence agencies in Timor-Leste at the height of the terror threat to Australian citizens is baffling. It was John Howard's Coalition government that sanctioned the reported Australian Secret Intelligence Service (ASIS) operation in impoverished Timor-Leste in 2004. It was Tony Abbott's Coalition government that authorised the Australian Security Intelligence Organisation and Australian Federal Police raids on Witness K's home and Bernard Collaery's office in 2013, and that was ordered by the International Court of Justice not to spy on Timor-Leste's lawyers when Timor-Leste sought return of the seized documents. It was the Turnbull Coalition government that approved the prosecutions in June 2018, and it is the Morrison Coalition government that is desperately trying to ensure Collaery's trial is held in secret.

Surely there are questions to be asked of the key players at the time of the alleged bugging: prime minister John Howard, foreign minister Alexander Downer and resources minister Ian Macfarlane (who, seven months after retiring from parliament in 2016, joined the board of Woodside). Equally, the current treasurer, Josh Frydenberg – who was an adviser to Downer from 1999 to 2003 and to Howard from 2003 to 2004 – and the member for Wentworth and former diplomat Dave Sharma – who was Downer's legal adviser from 2004 to 2006 – may be able to shed light on Australia's activities in Dili, if asked.

ALP senator Jenny McAllister's commentary on my essay does not address the Coalition's decades-long cover-up. She rightly calls out the Turnbull and Morrison governments' failures to implement the recommendations of the L'Estrange and Merchant 2017 Independent Intelligence Review on the oversight of Australia's ten intelligence agencies. A private member's bill McAllister introduced in 2019 seeks to implement some of the recommendations of the review, including allowing the Parliamentary Joint Committee on Intelligence and Security (PJCIS) to initiate inquiries without waiting for a referral from the prime minister, and to refer matters to the IGIS that the committee was not able to investigate itself. While any increase in oversight is better than none, McAllister's bill does not extend to giving the PJCIS the power to initiate inquiries into the legality and propriety of operational activities (such as spying on a friendly neighbour for economic gain while diverting resources from threats to Australian lives from terrorist activities).

Hewson, in contrast, calls for "more-effective scrutiny, from outside the executive, of our intelligence services and their operations". There is clearly need for reform. A research paper released by the Australia Institute in September found that "Australia's parliamentary oversight of its intelligence community is weak compared to that of other countries in the Five Eyes. Most significantly, parliamentarians in the UK, USA and Canada have oversight over the operations and activities of intelligence agencies, which Australia and New Zealand lack." Hewson argues the PJCIS should have complete access to intelligence briefings provided to government, and the powers of a royal commission to investigate possible illegalities. He also "strongly supports" historian Peter Edwards' call for the next intelligence review to be upgraded to a royal commission, as do I.

Andrew Zammit provides compelling reasons to include the Witness K scandal in the terms of reference of a royal commission, as I suggested. A commission could "help uncover the truth, rectify what appears to be a great injustice and address the scandal's impact on the public legitimacy of Australia's intelligence agencies".

Zammit's observation, as an expert on terrorism and security issues, that "the prosecutions perpetuate the scandal for ASIS" when "the intelligence agencies have an increasingly important role to play as global order deteriorates" is telling. Attorney-General Christian Porter and senior ASIS figures seemed determined to prosecute Collaery and Witness K regardless of the damage to ASIS's reputation and Australia's international standing, and to our relationship with Timor-Leste.

Hewson quotes lawyer and former senior federal public servant Ian Cunliffe, who comments that if the Commonwealth wants Collaery's "head on a platter", the Commonwealth "should be required to acknowledge its own crime in open court, and to defend its actions". However, in the Supreme Court of the Australian Capital Territory, the Commonwealth is doing everything it can to avoid confirming the spying occurred. Collaery is charged with one count of conspiring with Witness K to communicate information prepared by ASIS to the government of Timor-Leste, and four counts of communicating information prepared by ASIS to ABC journalists Emma Alberici, Peter Lloyd, Conor Duffy, Marian Wilkinson and producer Peter Cronau at various dates in 2013 and 2014. The attorney-general is seeking to publicly maintain a position of "neither confirming nor denying" the information Collaery and Witness K are charged with communicating.

On 26 June, Justice David Mossop ruled in the government's favour, finding that material Porter identified as sensitive should remain classified in Collaery's trial.

In the judgement – of which over a quarter is redacted – we learn that Porter sought orders that would "permit the evidence led by the Crown that establishes what part of the matters communicated by Mr Collaery were true, to be confined to those immediately involved in the case and not otherwise disclosed". In lay terms, this seems to mean that the jury would be made aware of the truth of the information Collaery imparted (for example, perhaps, communications about an ASIS Dili spying operation), but this confirmation would only happen in a hearing closed to the public. Denying the obvious is apparently necessary to protect Australia's national security.

This is absurd.

Collaery is appealing.

Kim McGrath is the author of Crossing the Line:
Australia's Secret History in the Timor Sea.

"Data Driven"
by Danielle Cave

Lesley Seebeck

anielle Cave's article "Data Driven" (AFA9: *Spy vs Spy*) does an excellent job of setting out a number of the challenges facing the collectors of intelligence in a technology-imbued, interconnected world. But technology has had perverse and insidious effects on the intelligence process even beyond the issues Cave describes.

Intelligence has been faced with many challenges over the last thirty years. In 1994, Joseph Nye wrote that, with the end of the Cold War, intelligence shifted from secrets to mysteries. It's one thing to pursue missile counts and sensor ranges – secrets – but entirely another to ascertain whether Boris Yeltsin can control inflation.

The 9/11 attacks on the United States in 2001 altered the frame again. Western intelligence agencies reeled from apparent failures in collection, analysis and coordination, exacerbated by the subsequent revelation that no weapons of mass destruction were found in Iraq. Their focus had to shift from established nation-states to an amorphous group of low-tech fighters in broken states. And they had to provide evidence, not simply reasoning borne from partial information and intuition.

Technology came to the fore in intelligence agencies. Mass information collection – sourcing reams of data – was less risky than the messy, difficult business of recruiting agents in unfamiliar environments. Data was traceable and verifiable – useful in legal prosecution – and it could be endlessly reanalysed. Combined with immense computational capability, it rendered possible the tedious task of finding tiny needles in huge haystacks, allowing America to exploit its position at the centre of the global internet and communications network.

As the threat from within – lone wolves, terrorists and hackers – came to dominate government attention, US internal security and law-enforcement agencies started to develop and borrow technologies and capabilities that were once the preserve of outward-looking foreign and defence intelligence agencies, turning them on their own populations.

The dangers of this technology-driven approach are manifold.

First, technology has encouraged notions of absolutism. As Cave notes, in the modern digital society little is exempt from mass collection. Both decision-makers and the public have come to expect immediacy and certainty. A lack of awareness of threats is considered unacceptable and, after an incident or an attack, unforgivable, driving agencies to seek out ever more intrusive surveillance in pursuit of exceptionally low signals in high levels of noise.

Second, mass collection reinforces the idea that more data is better. That's a trap: beyond a certain point, more data is simply more noise, with less clarity and more opportunities for misinterpretation, as American mathematician and cryptographer Claude E. Shannon noted in 1948. The answers to secrets and mysteries do not leap, fully formed, from the raw data; typically, a framing question or concept is required. It's not more data we need, but more seasoned analysts armed with sharper questions to draw out key judgements to inform policy. As US intelligence analyst Zachery Tyson Brown observed in February 2020, "consumers of intelligence are drowning in data, but thirsting for insight".

Third, digital technology, especially its reach and speed, disrupts the traditional roles in the intelligence process. The precarious stability of the Cold War refined the intelligence cycle: establish requirements in response to policy questions, undertake collection, analyse the take and disseminate assessments to policymakers. Now, policymakers reach straight to collectors and form their own judgements, often without the context provided by separate intelligence analysis.

Fourth, digital technologies create unhelpful intelligence rivalries. Not only do assessment agencies find themselves bit players, but the community as a whole is competing with wealthier actors with greater capabilities and reach. Large tech platforms such as Google, Facebook and Twitter engage in the same process of mass collection, analysis and sharing, crowdsourcing insights and tailoring responses to consumer preferences. Decision-makers are inundated with social media opinion and online commentary, which are often more immediately accessible than intelligence. Algorithms, fake news and disinformation, which also shape the operating environment, if not the actual decisions, of policymakers can make it harder for assessment agencies and their careful, objective reasoning to be heard.

Last, Cave's article raises questions about the purpose of intelligence. After all, if all queries can be googled or crowdsourced – or information corrupted – then what is the value of intelligence? And if statecraft rests on knowledgeable, objective insight and judgement about the external environment based on national interests, how can this be attained in a technologically driven world?

There are no easy solutions here. But informed intelligence is needed more than ever in a disruptive and increasingly contested global environment. Asking the right questions and examining the influence that technology is having on our perceptions of information-gathering and on our intelligence agencies, as Cave has begun to do, is a promising start.

Professor Lesley Seebeck is the CEO of the Cyber Institute
at the Australian National University.

Olivia Shen

Danielle Cave's essay thoughtfully examines the pain points that are driving intelligence agencies towards a new kind of tradecraft. In a world of big data, the intelligence community needs to be faster and more persuasive, agile enough to pivot to urgent "black swans" while maintaining coverage of long-term priorities and more mundane, predictable events.

While Cave is spot-on about spycraft becoming increasingly data-driven, it is worth unpacking what this means in practice for Australian intelligence agencies, especially as they balance the roles of humans versus advanced machines.

Spies may benefit from having more data at their disposal, but data can also add layers of complexity and difficulty to intelligence collection and analysis. How do you parse increasingly large amounts of information to find *insight*? As cryptographer and security expert Bruce Schneier puts it, when your mission is to find the needle in the haystack, the solution is not adding more hay.

Our key intelligence competitor, China, might disagree. China has effectively industrialised mass surveillance and data mining. With security cameras on every street corner, consumer data collected through every app, and cybersecurity laws giving pervasive powers to the state, China vacuums up enormous caches of data daily. Based on estimates from its Academy of Sciences, China currently holds 20 per cent of global data, or forty-four billion terabytes.

The sheer scale of this data collection raises concerns about "techno-authoritarianism" and the impact of data-driven technologies on privacy and human rights. China's government has already weaponised data against the

Uighur and Kazakh populations in Xinjiang Province. Worryingly, China is increasingly expanding or exporting these tools of social control.

Australian intelligence agencies cannot perform such wholesale data collection. Our agencies are subject to more stringent accountability standards and legal constraints. Even if Australia's collection capabilities were to reach the same level as China's, it is hard to see us trampling our values to copy China's playbook.

If intelligence agencies cannot best China on data collection, they might still gain an edge through better analysis. Cave predicts that over the next decade, agencies will spend much of their time figuring out how to host, process and use data, which only offers value if it can be properly analysed.

China has invested heavily in artificial intelligence for data analysis, boasting that it has built machine-learning algorithms capable of accurately sensing and predicting criminal behaviours and national security threats. AI has the added benefit of being able to process information at lightning speeds without fatigue, unlike the human intelligence collector or analyst.

However, the deployment of AI for intelligence analysis has its own pitfalls. AI's outputs are not always as accurate as they purport to be. From racist facial recognition to sexist credit scores, examples of algorithmic bias have been widely reported in recent years. Often these biases stem from flawed data used in the training of AI systems. It is an important reminder that data needs to be fit for purpose – it must be reliable and relevant for the specific dilemma that the AI is trying to solve. Complex AI systems, such as deep neural networks, can also present a "black box problem" where the AI's outputs cannot be fully dissected and explained. Biased or unexplainable AI is unlikely to deliver intelligence that convinces decision-makers.

We ought to imagine a future intelligence community that combines the best elements of both human and machine to wrangle data and make better-informed decisions. This will entail greater investment in tools and technologies, especially AI, but also the workforce capabilities to harness data effectively and avoid AI pitfalls. So-called "soft" sciences – linguistics, sociology, anthropology, history – are critical for transforming data into insight. Take languages as the most basic example. There is a joke among China watchers: "What's China's first layer of encryption? Write it in Chinese."

Spycraft will never be solely data-driven. Having the right human in the driver's seat is more important than ever.

Olivia Shen is a policy adviser, a Fulbright scholar and a former visiting scholar at the Center for Strategic and International Studies in Washington, DC.

Peter Rogers

ntelligence agencies undoubtedly need to adapt if they want to operate successfully in an endless sea of data. They are facing new challenges – like COVID-19 – but, as per the warnings of speculative fiction, intelligence must be tempered by a nuanced understanding of the order being protected. This has been the subject of speculation since Yevgeny Zamyatin's *We* and Jack London's *The Iron Heel* laid the groundwork for George Orwell's dystopian vision of the future in *Nineteen Eighty-Four*. While we are not, perhaps yet, sleepwalking into a world of total surveillance and repressive control, democratic nations are increasingly placing limits on freedom in the pursuit of order.

Danielle Cave discusses several technical challenges to the mining, scraping and hoovering up of open-source content from a digital world, but largely omits the ethical issues. Unprecedented access to data raises questions about our rights as citizens. Public and private organisations can now access a wide range of information about us, often *without* our direct knowledge and *with* our tacit consent. We rarely realise the access we give away when accepting terms and conditions to download a smartphone app, to join a public wi-fi network or to auto top-up cash on a travel card. The means by which data is gathered and used must be better understood and better overseen. To evoke Cave: "The complexities of this relationship won't change anytime soon. Our political leaders need to learn how to talk about it."

Data gathered by smart apps can improve decision-making. It can, for instance, help city planners ensure that the traffic system copes with evacuation routes in times of crisis. But the same tools can enable covert tracking – easily achieved by cross-referencing a live feed from a CCTV camera with facial recognition software. Real-time tracking can also occur through almost any wi-fi device without our knowledge. If you leave the wi-fi 'turned on' your device will be actively scanning for nearby connections, which means your device transmits a probe request to available networks nearby. In this probe is a unique hardware identifier, called a MAC address, allowing anyone who can "see" the signal to access the unique hardware code, identifying the owner. Cross-reference the appearance of that address on other network towers, and anyone with access can effectively track where a person is and has been. These technologies, already in use to enforce quarantine compliance during the COVID-19 pandemic, raise concerns about privacy, as well as the right to free movement and free association. Legislative, regulatory and other safeguards must adequately protect citizen rights, particularly from government attempts to "nudge" behaviours and from exploitation by for-profit interests.

The Institute for Governance and Policy Analysis report *Democracy 2025* shows that trust in Australia's democratic institutions is declining. As trust in the state diminishes, safeguards for citizen rights become essential. We must have confidence that our digital footprint is not abused in the name of intelligence-gathering or national security from never-ending crises.

At least sixty countries have adopted a digital tracking and tracing system during the COVID-19 pandemic. In almost all cases there have been concerns over the collection, storage and appropriate use of this data. There is a need to ensure that only necessary data is collected, for scientifically valid reasons, and that collection, analysis and storage is limited to the duration of the crisis. The invasive nature of these apps abrogates rights such as privacy, which is protected only by a loose covenant of general guidance rather than by specific laws.

Privacy must become a collective right in this age of information. It is weakened by the phishing, tracking, tracing and scraping of data, lauded by Cave as essential for the business of "intelligence".

Researchers into algorithmic governance are increasingly concerned that machine learning and predictive analytics are changing our daily lives. As Cave notes, use of these technologies is only going to increase. They are more and more embedded in how we live, buy, shop, learn, communicate and participate in our democracy. The technical challenges cannot trump the ethical challenges in understanding how this will shape democratic systems of social ordering. People are already rebelling against biometric surveillance with masks and reflective make-up to prevent unwanted potential tracking.

While information gathered about us might help govern during a crisis, we cannot accept this as "business as usual". In a post-COVID world, the gathering and use of data will only deepen; it must be tempered by safeguards against abuse or we may yet lose our personal freedom to a digital cage of information.

Dr Peter Rogers is a senior lecturer in
sociology at Macquarie University.

Danielle Cave responds

I wrote the bulk of my essay "Data Driven" before work, with a grumpy six-month-old either snoring or screaming nearby. There was sleep deprivation, too much caffeine and plenty of anxiety about what to include – and what not to include – given the word limit. Engaging with these thoughtful responses to my essay is helpful – it forces me to remember why, and what, I deliberately pushed aside or shaved off along the way.

Lesley Seebeck, Olivia Shen and Peter Rogers reveal how much more there is to unpack when it comes to the world's intelligence communities and how they are engaging with, and being reshaped by, cyberspace, data and, increasingly, technology. Seebeck in particular makes some excellent points about the dangers of a technology-driven intelligence process. In this, she essentially outlines an entirely different essay that could, and should, be written.

Both Seebeck ("It's not more data we need, but more seasoned analysts") and Chen ("Spycraft will never be solely data-driven") make the case that people are more vital than ever in assessing intelligence. I couldn't agree more. Data is useless if you don't have the right combination of specialists to draw insights from it. Intelligence communities will forever have to balance their investment in the collection process and in the analysts needed to draw insights and make judgements from that collection.

My own centre at the Australian Strategic Policy Institute (ASPI) provides a good example of just how important people are in the process of information collection and assessment, although the information we collect is far more public than that of intelligence agencies. A report published by ASPI's International Cyber Policy Centre can now attract a readership of hundreds of thousands. Most of these reports are the result of small teams of analysts working together for months to slowly, manually build up datasets that can be used to under-pin analysis and policy recommendations. These datasets don't yet exist in the open-source environment (and often, we're told, can't be found in classified environments, either). Complicated datasets are hard to build, and even harder to assess, requiring the right combination of specialists who possess language skills and deep country and/or thematic expertise. Few advanced machines or artificial intelligence systems have proven useful here. While investments in new technologies are essential, this doesn't diminish the importance of individ-uals. As Chen points out, "Having the right human in the driver's seat is more important than ever."

But intelligence communities need to invest in more than "seasoned analysts". I'd argue that it's equally vital to invest in the unseasoned (and great things can come from pairing the two). To draw on another example from my day job, some of the institute's most-read and impactful reports and blog posts are written by three employees – all with very different backgrounds and a com-bined age of less than seventy-five. These three analysts are many things, but "seasoned" they are not!

Rogers makes some interesting points, especially on data privacy and ethics. The Australian public should expect, and demand, that ethics be infused into all facets of how their government engages the world – across diplomacy, defence and intelligence. Some intelligence communities, for example, now employ ethics advisers to provide guidance on different operational aspects to their work. One can see such advisers and debates about ethics becoming more central in today's intelligence agencies.

But for the most part, Rogers misunderstands my essay. It is not about the targeting of Australians and the collection of their data by our government or the private sector – as deserving as these topics may be of further attention. Rather, my piece explores how governments around the world engage in for-eign intelligence collection, and in particular how cyberspace, the proliferation of data and emerging technologies are affecting that collection, and the work of the analysts who write it up.

I certainly don't believe and did not say, as Rogers implies, that it should be "business as usual" to collect the private data of Australians during a crisis. But I do believe that open-source intelligence collection, which all governments engage in, can provide useful and timely insights. It's worth noting that academics and journalists also engage in open-source intelligence collection. It just has a different name: research and investigation. My original point, about the analysis of Chinese social media data during the early days of what became the COVID-19 pandemic, was based on work published by Xi'an Jiaotong University's Department of Infectious Diseases. And it is universities, across the world, that have built, and continue to host, some of the best Chinese social media analytical tools.

Seebeck quotes US intelligence analyst Zachery Tyson Brown, who said that "consumers of intelligence are drowning in data, but thirsting for insight". It's also important to note that this thirst exists outside the intelligence community. Never has the world had access to so much information.

But have we invested enough, and in the right ways, to ensure we have sufficient people analysing this information in useful ways? I'd argue no, given that so much of the research produced by countries emerges from universities and is siphoned off into the world of academic publishing. Journal articles and monographs aren't especially accessible to the general public; nor are they always useful to those outside of narrow academic fields. Cordoning new and valuable knowledge remains an enormous opportunity cost. Seebeck's argument that "informed intelligence is needed more than ever in a disruptive and increasingly contested global environment" can be extended. Informed analysis – whether classified or unclassified – is needed more than ever.

My essay is thoroughly referenced, though the journal does not publish these references in its pages, and the overwhelming majority of my sources were from the United States – investigative journalists, think-tankers, academics and material from the intelligence agencies themselves. This served as a reminder about how little public discussion, analysis and reporting there is in Australia on intelligence issues. If it wasn't for the plethora of public reporting and official commentary continuously emerging from the United States, and the sprinkling from the United Kingdom (where spy chiefs increasingly give media interviews outlining their priorities), there would have been very little for me to write.

But things are changing. Some Australian spy chiefs, and their agencies, are slowly coming out of the shadows, led by Mike Burgess, former director-general of the Australian Signals Directorate (ASD) and now head of ASIO, who has given a number of public speeches and oversaw the launch of Twitter accounts at both agencies. In September 2020, the new director-general of the ASD, Rachel Noble, gave her first major public speech, at the Australian National University. Days before, her US counterpart, Paul M. Nakasone, commander of US Cyber Command and director of the National Security Agency, co-authored an essay in US journal *Foreign Affairs* titled "How to Compete in Cyberspace".

There is a gap in Australian public discourse when it comes to intelligence issues, and Australia would benefit from more journalists, think-tankers and academics reporting on, writing about and debating these issues. And perhaps *Australian Foreign Affairs* could pull together some of our spy chiefs for a special edition that would help fill this void.

Danielle Cave is deputy director of the International Cyber Policy Centre at the Australian Strategic Policy Institute.

"Party Faithful"
by Anne-Marie Brady

Alex Joske

Professor Anne-Marie Brady's essay on China's spies (AFA9: *Spy vs Spy*) comes as the "hidden battlefront" – to use one of the Chinese Communist Party's favoured terms for covert work – is being forced into the spotlight. Hong Kong's new state security office represents the first official presence of China's intelligence agencies in the region. In July, the US government ordered China to close its consulate in Houston, Texas, alleging it was a hotbed of espionage. Weeks later, a former CIA officer was charged with working for China's Ministry of State Security. Growing tensions with Beijing have come as governments around the world refresh and expand their counterintelligence capabilities.

Despite the proliferation of cases linked to China's intelligence agencies, very little is known about these agencies publicly. There are few researchers outside of government who specialise in this area. Accurate information is hard to come by, and even harder to unearth. The Chinese military's Political Work Department Liaison Bureau – one of the Party's most important interference and espionage agencies – doesn't even have its own Wikipedia page. In 2012, Andrew Forrest and former China ambassador Geoff Raby were pictured with the agency's head, who was operating through one of its front groups. With notable exceptions such as Peter Mattis and Matthew Brazil's *Chinese Communist Espionage* and Michael Schoenhals's *Spying for the People*, books and essays on the Party's intelligence work are often unreliable and woefully incomplete. Indictments from China-linked espionage cases are an important resource in finding out and establishing more about the Party's inner workings.

This lack of reliable and accessible material on the Party's intelligence work presents a challenge to Brady's exhortation that "knowledge of Chinese intelligence agencies should be a standard feature of the workplace education of politicians, diplomats and other public servants".

Brady's essay itself demonstrates the depth of this knowledge gap. I can't confirm its claim that the Ministry of State Security (MSS), China's primary civilian intelligence organisation, was recently split into separate counterintelligence and foreign intelligence agencies. The theory traces back to a Hong Kong media report that has not been substantiated. The essay's description of bureaus under the MSS has its origins in decades-old Taiwanese government information. This leads to the essay's reference to the "Enterprises Division", a bureau that probably no longer exists, and an erroneous description of an "Imaging Intelligence Division" as the MSS's cyberespionage bureau.

Details such as the responsibilities of different MSS bureaus are time-consuming to uncover. For most politicians, diplomats and public servants, the key will instead be understanding what distinguishes the Party's intelligence work from Western preconceptions of spying.

In this context, Brady rightly draws attention to the CCP's bureaucratic systems. These are groupings of agencies around functional lines, such as foreign affairs, united front work and propaganda, that coordinate across the bureaucracy and ensure directives are implemented. They are an important feature of the party-state's bureaucracy, highlighting how dozens of agencies can work under common guidance and objectives.

The picture isn't as straightforward with China's intelligence agencies. The split between military and civilian intelligence agencies means they may not be as coordinated at the top. Still, the idea that different arms of the Party contribute to intelligence work is important.

While Brady characterises two of those Party organs as "intelligence agencies", it's important to highlight that their work is distinct from, yet integrated with, intelligence.

For example, the United Front Work Department's focus on building and managing networks of Party-aligned groups and individuals is complementary to intelligence work. This activity can be both overt and covert. United front networks can be a way for the Party to mobilise overseas communities for cultural events. They also enable recruitment and intelligence gathering. Examples of Chinese espionage from Hong Kong and Taiwan, as well as Western cases such as that of Katrina Leung, who was accused of handing FBI secrets to Beijing, demonstrate how widespread this practice is.

In a 1939 politburo meeting, Zhou Enlai, the father of China's United Front and intelligence systems, advocated "nestling intelligence within the United Front". In other words, united front work is also designed to serve as cover or noise in which clandestine activity can hide. But the two kinds of activity are distinct.

This little-understood nexus of united front work and intelligence work often manifests as political interference. A search warrant from the ongoing investigation into John Zhang, a former staffer to New South Wales politician Shaoquett Moselmane, highlighted this. The warrant accused him of working on behalf of both the MSS and the United Front Work Department. Similarly, the case of defector Wang Liqiang, who claimed to have worked in a political interference network involving a university alumni association, an education charity, media executives and two listed companies, points to such "nestling".

A country's understanding of the interweaving of united front work and intelligence work will shape its response to China's operations. Australia's response to these threats focuses on interference and espionage, and rightly distinguishes between influence and interference – the latter a covert, corrupting or coercive subset of influence. But the Party's efforts involve "using the legal to mask the illegal; deftly integrating the legal and the illegal", to quote Zhou Enlai again. In fact, one emblem the MSS uses includes a symbol believed to represent the integration of covert and overt work, of black and white. This mismatch between China's activities and our responses creates a serious challenge that all democracies are forced to navigate.

Alex Joske is an analyst at the Australian Strategic
Policy Institute's International Cyber Policy Centre.

Anne-Marie Brady responds

I t is great to receive feedback on my article "Party Faithful".

I scoured every available public source on China's party, state and military intelligence organisations to write the piece. I am grateful for Alex Joske for adding in some extra details, which were not available to me at the time of writing. These additions are very important to mainstream knowledge of how intelligence agencies work in China.

I hope that more authors will take up the challenge to shine a light on this area of Chinese politics.

Anne-Marie Brady is a professor at the University of Canterbury and a global fellow at the Wilson Center in Washington, DC.

Subscribe to Australian Foreign Affairs & save up to 28% on the cover price.

Enjoy free home delivery of the print edition and full digital as well as ebook access to the journal via the Australian Foreign Affairs website, iPad, iPhone and Android apps.

Forthcoming issue:
The March of Autocracy
(February 2021)

Never miss an issue. Subscribe and save.

☐ **1 year auto-renewing print and digital subscription** (3 issues) $49.99 within Australia. Outside Australia $79.99*.

☐ **1 year print and digital subscription** (3 issues) $59.99 within Australia. Outside Australia $99.99.

☐ **1 year auto-renewing digital subscription** (3 issues) $29.99.*

☐ **2 year print and digital subscription** (6 issues) $114.99 within Australia.

☐ Tick here to commence subscription with the current issue.

Give an inspired gift. Subscribe a friend.

☐ **1 year print and digital gift subscription** (3 issues) $59.99 within Australia. Outside Australia $99.99.

☐ **1 year digital-only gift subscription** (3 issues) $29.99.

☐ **2 year print and digital gift subscription** (6 issues) $114.99 within Australia.

☐ Tick here to commence subscription with the current issue.

ALL PRICES INCLUDE GST, POSTAGE AND HANDLING.

*Your subscription will automatically renew until you notify us to stop. Prior to the end of your subscription period, we will send you a reminder notice.

Please turn over for subscription order form, or subscribe online at **australianforeignaffairs.com**
Alternatively, call 1800 077 514 or +61 3 9486 0288 or email **subscribe@australianforeignaffairs.com**

Back Issues

ALL PRICES INCLUDE
GST, POSTAGE
AND HANDLING.

☐ **AFA1** ($15.99)
The Big Picture

☐ **AFA2** ($15.99)
Trump in Asia

☐ **AFA3** ($15.99)
Australia & Indonesia

☐ **AFA4** ($15.99)
Defending Australia

☐ **AFA5** ($15.99)
Are We Asian Yet?

☐ **AFA6** ($15.99)
Our Sphere of Influence

☐ **AFA7** ($15.99)
China Dependence

☐ **AFA8** ($22.99)
Can We Trust America?

☐ **AFA9** ($22.99)
Spy vs Spy

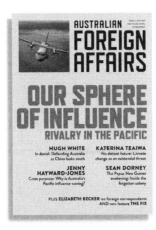

PAYMENT DETAILS I enclose a cheque/money order made out to Schwartz Books Pty Ltd.
Or please debit my credit card (MasterCard, Visa or Amex accepted).

CARD NO. ☐☐☐☐ ☐☐☐☐ ☐☐☐☐ ☐☐☐☐

EXPIRY DATE ___ / ___ CCV _____ AMOUNT $ _____

CARDHOLDER'S NAME _____

SIGNATURE _____

NAME _____

ADDRESS _____

EMAIL _____ PHONE _____

Post or fax this form to: Reply Paid 90094, Carlton VIC 3053 **Freecall:** 1800 077 514 **or** +61 3 9486 0288
Fax: (03) 9011 6106 **Email:** subscribe@australianforeignaffairs.com **Website:** australianforeignaffairs.com
Subscribe online at australianforeignaffairs.com/subscribe (please do not send electronic scans of this form)

The Back Page

NETPOLITIK

What is it: A supposedly new style of diplomacy that seeks "to exploit the powerful capabilities of the internet to shape politics, culture, values, and personal identity". It was coined by David Bollier (founder, Commons Strategies Group) after an Aspen Institute conference in 2002. He claimed it would be the successor to realpolitik.

Was it right: Although a prescient term, it has not gained wide currency in foreign policy circles. Similar terminology has been used for adjacent phenomena: *mediapolitik* (politics shaped by mass media), *cyberpolitik* (the diplomacy of cyberattacks and information technology) and *noopolitik* (a form of statecraft focused on the use and denial of information).

Was it wrong: The internet was a sunnier place in 2002. The Aspen crowd believed netpolitik – in contrast to the "amoral coercion" of realpolitik – would traffic in soft-power issues, "such as moral legitimacy, cultural identity, societal values, and public perception". Instead, the internet has become another frontier of realpolitik, and a means of creating amoral coercion – or, as Mark Zuckerberg (CEO, Facebook) put it, "doing sketchy things".

Politiks as usual: Much of the vocabulary of modern diplomacy comes from nineteenth-century Europe, an era of emerging and competing nationalisms. *Realpolitik* originates here. The most lasting, *geopolitik* – which became "geopolitics" – was devised by a Swede, Rudolf Kjellén (Skyttean Professor, Uppsala University), who also created two other terms with far-reaching foreign policy consequences: *Volk* and *Reich*.